INST*A*
PORTU_

by Dorothy Thomas

Editorial consultant and translator
Lata Jamieson
Assisted by
Raquel Marques

Illustrated by DRAGONFLY DESIGNS

apropos design

dot publications

The first trip for this book to the Minho coincided with a heatwave, making any research except into sources of refreshment impossible. All pretence at work was therefore abandoned. Later investigations ranged from Bragança to the Alentejo and parts in between, including sampling every form of transport in Lisbon from the Tejo ferries to trams and funiculars and the French-designed, British-built street lift, the Elevador Santa Justa in the Chiado.

Dorothy Thomas studied at the Universities of Newcastle upon Tyne, Oslo and Bonn and is a member of the Institute of Linguists. She works as a teacher and translator and specialises in Norwegian.

Grateful thanks are due to the author's collaborators Lata Jamieson and Raquel Marques, especially in the quagmire of pronunciation.

First published 1994
Copyright © DM Thomas 1994

Published by dot Publications
54A Haig Avenue, Whitley Bay, NE25 8JD, Great Britain

ISBN 1 871086 07 8

All rights reserved. No part of this book may be reproduced or transmitted in any form or by any means, electronic or mechanical, including photocopying, recording, or by any information storage and retrieval system without permission in writing from the Publisher

Produced by Roger Booth Associates, Newcastle upon Tyne
Printed in the U.K. by Bell & Bain Ltd., Glasgow

PORTUGAL

Coimbra	–	**Kweem**bra
Estoril	–	Stor-**eel**
Guimarães	–	Gheema-**rangsh**
Lagos	–	**Laag**oosh
Portimão	–	Portee-**mowng**
Setúbal	–	**Shtoo**bal

o BRASIL

Rio de Janeiro	–	**Ree**-oo duh Zhuh**nay**roo
Belém	–	Buh-**leng**
São Paulo	–	Sowng **Pow**-loo

Contents

Page

Colours	cover
Pronunciation	6
Accommodation	7
Eating out	16
Food shopping	23
Other shops	30
Bank, post office, telephone	35
Finding the way	39
Road travel	42
Public transport	50
Accidents and illness	57
Sightseeing, sport, entertainment	61
Making friends, visiting	64
Family, countries, nationalities	67
Pests, theft, lost property	68
Seasons, months, weather	69
Greetings, days, time of day	70
Time	71
Basic grammar	72
Portuguese index/food terms	74
English index	76
Numbers	80
Basic phrases	cover

Using this book

Even if you have never learnt another language, this book is designed to help you get by, so that you can get what you need or wherever you want to go.

Inside the back cover is a list of **basic phrases** which you can use in many different circumstances.

If you want a particular subject, first look it up in the **Contents** or the **Index** (pages 75-79). We take you through a series of typical tourist situations, giving you the words you need followed by some idea of the replies you are likely to hear. Follow the speech guide under each picture, stressing the syllables that are set in heavy type. The guide to **sounds** on page 6 will help you pronounce things correctly.

Most situations follow a basic pattern which you can use in different places. For example, the phrases used in the baker's on page 24 can be used in many other shops, too. Sentences are carefully designed to be interchangeable, so if you want something different from what is being asked for in the picture, you just slot it in.

Food/Portuguese index: on pages 74–75 there is a separate glossary of food items under their Portuguese names, plus a few other Portuguese terms.

In the **Index** you will sometimes find words included that are different from but related to the ones listed. For example, included under *nice* you will find page 22 where *very good* is used, as well as *lovely* on page 64.

If you want to find out more about the language works, on pages 72-73 is a short section that will give you an insight into Portuguese **grammar**.

Right at the back on page 80 is a list of **numbers**. Do learn these - numbers are a vital part of any language and will make it much easier to go shopping or make any sort of arrangements.

Remember, travelling should be fun. If you can talk to people and understand some of the signs you'll enjoy it much more. Since it's not common for foreigners to speak Portuguese, your efforts will be much appreciated. Don't be shy, have a go!

Enjoy yourself - and have a good trip - *Boa viagem!*

Portuguese sounds

We have tried to keep our transcription simple so that you can read the questions and answers almost as if they were English. Some words are split by a hyphen to make them easier to read and to get the stress in the right place; pronounce them as one word, with no gaps. **a** and **e** are often just a very short **uh**, like **a** in balloon or **e** in open (represented by '). Like English but unlike other Romance languages, **a** at the end of words is also **uh**, like **a** in china, or it may be almost inaudible. In fact, the Portuguese often seem to swallow their vowels while Brazilian speech is clearer.

a – *open* as in mat: f**a**lo (I speak);
– *closed* or *unstressed* like **u** in but or **a** in canoe: p**a**ra (for), M**a**deira.
e – as in let: jan**e**la (window); *closed* like **a** in say: p**e**lo (hair);
– *unstressed* as in spok**e**n or like **a** in canoe: s**e**mana *(s'maana*-week);
– often disappears at beginning of a word, or like **i** in immense: **e**stação (station).
i – like **ee** in bee but short: v**i** (I saw).
o – *open* like **a** in call: b**o**lo (cake); *closed* like **o** in note: h**o**mem (man);
– *unstressed* like **o** in too: livr**o** (book), bol**o** (cake).
u – like **oo** in too: ch**u**va (it's raining).
c – as in car, but before **e** or **i** or with a cedilla (**ç**), like **c** in ceiling.
ch – like **sh** in shoe: **ch**amar (to call), a**ch**o que sim (I think so).
g – as in go: **g**ato (cat); before **e** and **i** like **s** in measure: **g**elo (ice);
gu – before **a** like **gw**: **Gu**arda; **e** and **i** as in go: **gu**erra (war), **gu**itarra (guitar).
h – is silent: **h**á (there is/are).
j – like **s** in measure: **j**ogo (game).
lh – like **lli** in million: mu**lh**er (woman, wife).
nh – like **ni** in onion: vi**nh**o (wine).
qu – before **a** as in quality: **qu**atro (four); before **e** and **i**, like **c** in car: a**qu**i (here); exception: in cin**qu**enta (fifty) it's pronounced as in **qu**ality.
r – as in road: p**r**eço (price); rolled at beginning of a word or doubled: **r**io (river).
s – at the beginning of a word or doubled, like **s** in sit: **s**anto (holy), a**ss**ado (roast);
– between vowels like **z**: ca**s**a (house);
– at the end or between a vowel and a consonant, like **sh**: mê**s** (month), e**s**tá (is).
x – at the beginning of a word, before a consonant, and sometimes between vowels, it's like **sh**: **x**adrez (chess), bai**x**o (low), cai**x**a (cashier);
– between two vowels like **ss**: pró**x**imo (next), trou**x**e (I/he/she brought);
– when **ex** precedes a vowel, like **z**: e**x**acto *(eezaatoo*-exact); e**x**emplo (example);
– occasionally like **ks**: fi**x**o (fixed), tá**x**i (taxi).
z – beginning of word or in the middle, **z**: **z**ero (zero), ve**z**es *(vayzush*-times);
– at the end of a word like **s** in measure: ve**z** *(vayzh*-time), talve**z** (perhaps).

Stress This usually falls on the last syllable but one: passa**po**rte (passport). This also applies when two vowels are combined: pastela**ri**a (cake shop), conti**nu**a (it continues). Other words are stressed on the last syllable: a**qui** (here), ho**tel** (hotel). An accent on a syllable shows that it is stressed: far**má**cia (chemist), ma**çã** (apple).

Nasal sounds (e.g. English *sing*, French *bon*). Any vowel with ~ above it is nasal, as are vowels preceding **m** or **n**: banco-*bangkoo*, homem-*omeng* (the final **m** is silent). Vowels followed by **m** or **n** + a consonant are also nasal: Sesimbra, Benfica.

Booking accommodation

Exmo. Sr.,   Dear Sir,

Hotels:
Queria reservar um quarto individual (dois quartos individuais)
I should like to book one single room (two single rooms)

um/dois quarto/s de casal
one/two double room/s

com casa de banho/duche   *para — noite/s de — até — .*
with bath/shower   for — night/s from — to — .

Que quantia desejam como depósito para a reserva de quarto/s?
How much deposit is required to book the room/s?

Camping:
Queria reservar um lugar (com electricidade) no vosso parque de campismo,
à sombra se possível. Desejamos ficar — noites de — até — .

I should like to book a pitch (with electricity) on your campsite, in the shade if possible. We wish to stay — nights from — to — .

Temos um carro/uma roulotte/uma carrinha-cama
We have a car/caravan/motor caravan

e uma tenda grande/pequena (com toldo).
and a large/small tent (with awning).

No nosso grupo (na nossa família) há — adultos e — criança (crianças) de — anos de idade.
In our group (in our family) there are — adults and — child (children) aged — .

Que quantia desejam como depósito para a reserva do lugar?
How much deposit do you require to reserve the pitch?

                       *   *   *

Fazia-nos o favor de nos enviar as vossas tarifas.
Please let us know your rates.

Muito atenciosamente, sou,
Yours faithfully,

8 Hotels

Hotels, Motels and the state-run *Pousadas* all provide full board. A *Pensão* or an *Estalagem* always serves breakfast but may not offer other meals. At a *Residência* only breakfast is available. If you want a room, look for *quartos* or *dormidas*. Prices are always quoted per room, not per person.

If you've booked

1. Boa tarde.
2. Boa tarde.
3. Tenho um quarto reservado em nome de Jones.
4. Ah, sim, perfeitamente. O seu passaporte, se faz favor. Podia assinar aqui?

1. *Boa tard.*
    Good evening.
3. *Tainyoo oong kwartoo r'zer-vaadoo eng nawm duh Jones.*
    I have booked a room in the name of Jones.
2. *Boa tard.*
    Good evening.
4. *Ah, sing, purfaita-ment. Oo sayoo passa-port, s'fash fuh-vor. Poo-deeya ussee-nar uh-kee?*
    Yes, of course. May I have your passport? Please sign here.

If you haven't booked and the receptionist says, 'Está cheio' *(shta shay-oo)*, it's full. To ask if there is another hotel nearby; 'Há outro hotel aqui perto?' *(A awtroo oh-tel uh-kee pairtoo?)*

This sign is for the Tourist Office (**o Turismo**), who will often find you a hotel or private room.

Meals: *Dormida e pequeno almoço*
                           Bed & breakfast
                     (Br. *pernoite e café da manhã*)

Meia pensão   *Pensão completa*
Half board   Full board

Lift: *o Ascensor/Elevador*

Booking a room

1. *Boa tard. Teng oom **kwar**too purra shta noit?*
   Good evening. Have you a room for tonight?
3. *Purra ooma p'**saw**-a (**doo**-ush p'**saw**-ush) ee **doo**-ush kree-**ans**ush.*
   For one person (two) and two children.
5. *Purra ooma noit (ooma s'**maan**a).*
   For one night (a week).
2. *Sing, **tay**moosh. Purra **kwan**tush p'**saw**-ush?*
   Yes, how many for?
4. ***Mween**too beng. Purra **kwan**tush noitsh?*
   Fine. For how many nights?

1. *Pruh-**fair** oong **kwar**too duh k'**zaal** oh **eend**y-veed-**waal**?*
   Would you like a double room or a single?
3. *Kong kaaza d'**bun**yoo oh seng?*
   With bath or without?
2. *Oong duh k'**zaal** ee doish **eend**y-veedoo-**eye**sh.*
   A double and two singles.
4. *Kong kaaza d'**bun**yoo.*
   With bath.

com camas individuais – with twin beds

1. *Sing, **tay**moosh oong **kwar**too dishpoo-**nee**vel.*
   Yes, we have a room available.
2. ***Mween**too beng. **Kwan**too ay?*
   Good. How much is it?
3. *Sowng **kwat**roo meel **shkood**oosh poor noit.*
   It's 4000 escudos a night.
4. *Shta **beng**. **Kay**roo.*
   Fine. I'll take it.
5. *Awnd **paw**soo shtassyon-**ar**?*
   Where can I park?

1. *Beng. Oo **say**oo nawm, fash fuh-**vor**?*
   Good. What is your name, please?
2. *Oo **may**oo nawm ay Helen Baker.*
   My name is Helen Baker.
3. *Poo-**dee**ya m'dar oo **say**oo passa-**port**, s'fash fuh-**vor**?*
   Could you give me your passport, please?
4. ***Mween**too obry-**gaad**oo. Uh-**kee** teng uh soo-a shaav.*
   Thank you. Here is your key.

★ Chave número dezoito, faz favor.

*Shaav **noom**roo d'**zoi**too, fash fuh-**vor**.*
Key number 18, please.

3. *Eb-**bong**. **Kay**roo.*
   It's fine. I'll take it.
4. *Nowng, nowng **gawsh**too.
   Em-**ween**too burrool-**yent**oo
   (p'**ken**noo).*
   No, thanks, I don't like it. It's too noisy (small).
5. *No:·ng teng oong m'l-**yor**?*
   Have you anything better?
6. ***Seen**too **mween**too, nowng **tay**moosh.*
   I'm sorry, we haven't.

1. ***Sair**veng ruffay-**soingsh**?*
   Do you serve meals?
2. *Uh kee orush ay oo p'**ken**noo al-**moh**soo? (oo al-**moh**soo, oo zhan-**tar**)*
   What time is breakfast? (lunch, dinner)
3. *Dash **oit**oo ee maya ash desh.*
   From 8.30 to 10.

1. *Poo-**dee**ya m'**dar** uh kawnta, fash fuh-**vor**?*
   Could I have the bill, please?
2. *A-**day**oosh.*
   Goodbye.

(Time p.71, Paying p.33)

12 Rented accommodation

Finding your apartment

O apartamento (apto.) – the Apartment

You will usually know your host's name, so just ask:

Faz favor, podia-me dizer onde mora o senhor — (a senhora Dona —)?

Fash fuh-**vor**, poo-**dee**yam dee-**zair** awnd mora oo s'n-**yor** — (uh s'n-**yor**a dawna —)?

Excuse me, can you tell me where Mr — (Mrs —) lives?

A Cozinha   *uh koo-zeenya*   **The Kitchen**

- as chaves / ush shaavsh / the Keys
- o fogão / oo foo-**gowng** / the Cooker
- água quente/fria / aggwa kent/free-a / Hot/Cold Water
- a porta / uh porta / the Door
- o gás / oo gash / the Gas
- a electricidade / eelettreesy-**daad** / the Electricity

1. ... não funciona/está partido.
2. Quando é que o pode reparar?
3. Tem mais chávenas (outro cobertor)?

1. ... nowng foons-**yon**a/shta pur-**teed**oo.
   ... isn't working/is broken.
2. **Kwan**doo ay kuh oo pod ruppa-**rar**?
   When can you mend it?
3. Teng m-**eye**sh **shavv**nush (**aw**troo koobair-**tor**)?
   Have you any more cups (another blanket)?

| O Quarto / *oo kwartoo* / **The Bedroom** | as cortinas / *ush koor-teenush* / the Curtains | a luz / *uh loosh* / the Light | uma lâmpada / *ooma lampa-da* / a Light Bulb | A Casa de Banho / *uh kaaza d'bunyoo* / **The Bathroom** |

Os Lavabos / *oosh luh-vabboosh* / **The Lavatory/Toilet**

a torneira / *uh tor-nayra* / the Tap/Faucet

a janela / *uh zh'nella* / the Window

uma almofada / *ooma almoo-faada* / a Pillow

uma toalha / *ooma too-alya* / a Towel

a cama / *uh kumma* / the Bed

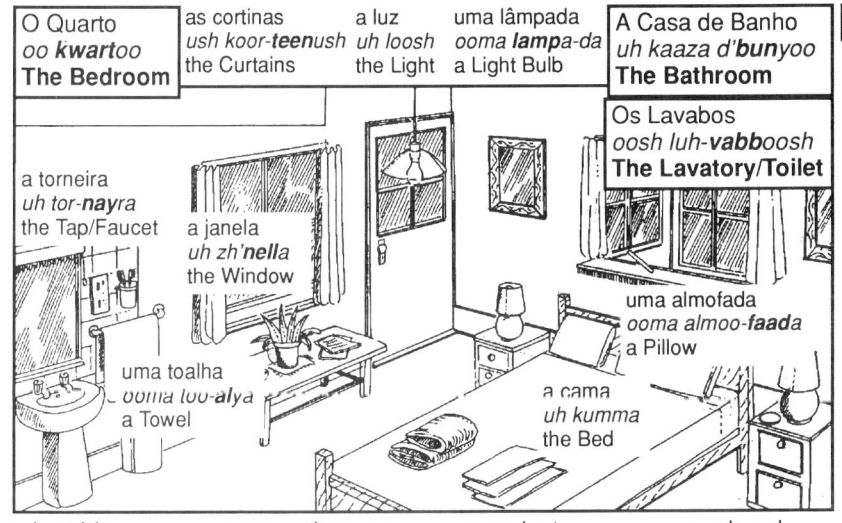

| o lavatório / *oo lavva-tory-oo* / the Basin | a roupa de cama / *uh ropa duh kumma* / the Bedclothes | um cobertor / *oong koobair tor* / a Blanket | um lençol / *oong leng-sol* / a Sheet |

| uma chávena / *ooma shavvna* / a Cup | um copo / *oong kawpoo* / a Glass | um prato / *oong praatoo* / a Plate | uma faca / *ooma faaka* / a Knife | um garfo / *oong garfoo* / a Fork | uma colher / *ooma kool-yair* / a Spoon |

uma panela / *ooma punnella* / a Saucepan

uma frigideira / *ooma freezhy-dayra* / a Frying Pan

o lixo / *oo leeshoo* / the Rubbish/Trash

| uma cadeira / *ooma kuh-dayra* / a Chair | a mesa / *uh maysa* / the Table | o lava-louça / *oo lavva loosa* / the Sink | uma cafeteira / *ooma kuffa-tayra* / a Coffee Pot |

| o frigorífico / *oo freegoo-reefy-koo* / the Fridge | *Br. a geladeira | um pano de loiça / *oong paanoo duh loisa* / a Tea-towel | um jarro / *oong zharroo* / a Jug |

CAMPING

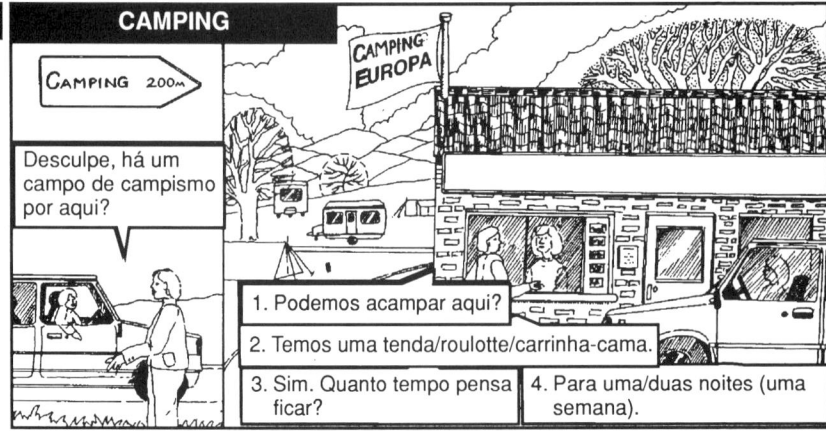

D'sh-koolp, a oong kampoo d'kam-peezhmoo poor uh-kee?
Excuse me, is there a campsite near here?

1. *Poo-daymoosh akkam-par uh-kee?*
   Hallo, can we camp here?
2. *Taymoosh ooma tenda/roo-lot/kur-reenya kumma.*
   We have a tent/caravan/motor caravan.
3. *Sing. Kwantoo taimpoo painsa fee-kar?*
   How long would you like to stay?
4. *Purra ooma/doo-ush noitsh (ooma s'maana).*
   One night/two (a week).

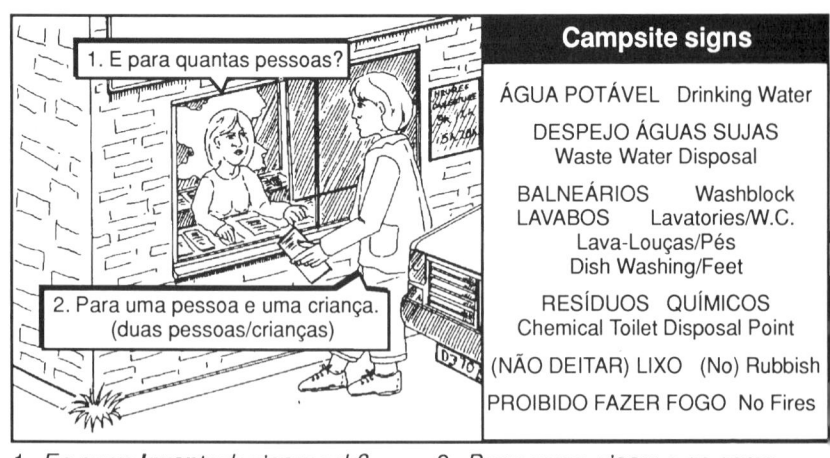

Campsite signs

ÁGUA POTÁVEL   Drinking Water

DESPEJO ÁGUAS SUJAS
Waste Water Disposal

BALNEÁRIOS   Washblock
LAVABOS   Lavatories/W.C.
Lava-Louças/Pés
Dish Washing/Feet

RESÍDUOS   QUÍMICOS
Chemical Toilet Disposal Point

(NÃO DEITAR) LIXO   (No) Rubbish

PROIBIDO FAZER FOGO   No Fires

1. *Ee purra kwantush p'saw-ush?*
   How many are there of you?
2. *Purra ooma p'saw-a ee ooma kree-ansa.*
   (doo-ush p'saw-ush/kree-ansush)
   One person and one child. (two people/children)

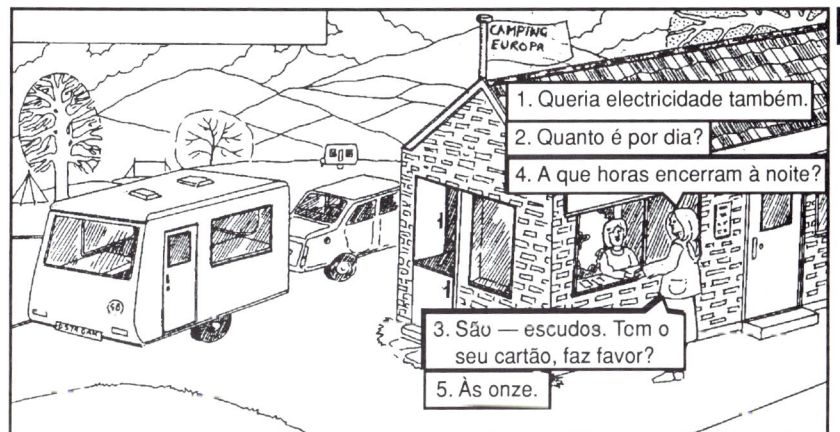

1. *Kree-a **ee**lettreesy-**daad** tam**beng**.*
   I'd like electricity, too.
2. ***Kwan**too ay poor dee-a?*
   How much is it per day?
4. *Uh kee **o**rush en-**serr**ang a noit?*
   What time do you close in the evening?
3. *Sowng — **shkood**oosh. Teng oo sayoo kur-**towng**, fash fuh-**vor**?*
   That will be — escudos. Have you a carnet, please?
5. *Ash awnz.*
   At eleven o'clock.

International camping carnet: Widely accepted at campsites overseas as an identity document. Though seldom obligatory, it's useful not to have to leave your passport in reception since you will also need it for changing money.

Proibido acampar – Não é permitido acampar aqui – No camping

Youth Hostel

o Albergue de Juventude
*al-**bairg** d'zhooven-**tood***
the Youth Hostel

1. *Boa noit. Teng **kumm**ush purra shta noit?*
   Hallo, have you any beds for tonight?
3. *Uh-**kee** shta oo **may**oo kur-**towng** dee al-**bairg**.*
   Here's my membership card.
2. *Sing, **tain**yoo. Purra **kwan**tush noitsh?*
   Yes, I have. How long for?

4. *Teng oong **sakk**oo duh door **meer**?*
   Have you got a sleeping bag?

Eating out

You won't go hungry in Brazil or Portugal at any time of day. All cafés serve coffee and snacks as well as soft drinks and alcohol, and most do meals. **Pousadas** also serve meals to non-residents, as do many **Pensões** (plural of *Pensão*). Look for signs saying **Comidas** (food), **Snack**, **Sandes** (sandwiches) or **Almoços e Jantares** (lunch and dinner). In Portugal the Menu is *a Ementa* or *a Lista*, while in Brazil it's known as *o Cardápio*. *Prato do dia* is the day's special. If you want to try something, ask for a portion – *uma dose ('dozz')*.

Horas de Abertura das 11.00h às 16.00h	– open from 11am to 4pm
Serve-se jantar a partir das 8.00h	– dinner served from 8 o'clock
Vende-se para fora	– food available to take away
Pão e manteiga	– cover charge: 'bread and butter'

Try these:
uma Cervejaria	– a large cafe or 'beer house'
uma Churrascaria	– grills, barbecues
uma Churrasqueira	– grills, especially chicken
uma Marisqueira	– a seafood restaurant
uma Pastelaria	– cakes and ice cream
um Restaurante	– a restaurant
um Salão de chá	– a 'tea room', also coffee and cakes

TIPPING? Service is usually included *(serviço incluído)*. If not, leave a few escudos or 10 per cent, depending on what you had.

MEALS: Breakfast is o pequeno almoço *(oo p'kennoo al-mohsoo)* in Portugal, o café da manhã *(oo kaf-fay dummun-yang)* in Brazil.

Lunch, o almoço *(oo al-mohsoo)*, is served from about 1.00 p.m.

Dinner, o jantar *(oo zhan-tar)*, is served from 8.00 p.m.

There's a sample menu on p.20, more meat p.26, fish p.27 and vegetables p.28. Food is listed separately at the front of the main index, pp.74-75.

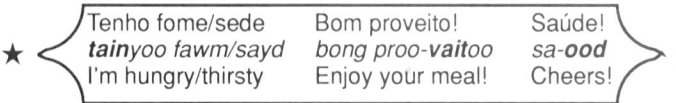

★ Tenho fome/sede — Bom proveito! — Saúde!
tainyoo fawm/sayd — bong proo-**vaitoo** — sa-**ood**
I'm hungry/thirsty — Enjoy your meal! — Cheers! ★

Basic ordering: drinks and snacks

Sandes/Sanduíches
sandsh/sandweeshs
  Sandwiches

um bolo
*oong
bawloo*
a Cake

uma cerveja
ooma s'vayzha
a Beer

um café/chá
com...
*kaf fay/sha
kong...*
a Coffee/Tea with...

leite/açúcar/gelo
layt/asookar/zhayloo
Milk/Sugar/Ice

um limão
oong lee-mowng
a Lemonade

uma laranja
ooma la-ranzha
an Orange Juice

um copo de
vinho —
*kawpoo
d'veenyoo*
a Glass of — Wine
(*tinto/branco:* red/white)

1. *Bong dee-a, kud-zayzhang?*
   Hello, what would you like?

4. *Taymoosh d'fee-ambr, kayzhoo ee shoreessoo. Tambeng taymoosh kuh-shorroosh ee am-boorgush.*
   We have ham, cheese and sausage. Also hot dogs and hamburgers.

3. *Kuh sand-weeshs teng? Ee awtrush koizush?*
   What sandwiches are there? Have you anything else?

2. *Kree-a ooma beeka, oong sha, ee oong soomoo dunna-nash.*
   I'd like an espresso coffee, a tea, and a pineapple juice.

Br. °*um cafezinho;* •*um suco;*
*presunto

Paying, finding the lavatory

1. *Shta ohkoo-paadoo?*
   Is this (seat/table) taken?

2. *Uh kawnta, s'fash fuh-vor*
   Could I have the bill, please.

3. *Awnd sowng oosh luh-vabboosh?*
   Where are the toilets?

Breakfast

1. *Olya, s'fash fuh-**vor**!*
   Excuse me, please.
4. *Poo-**dee**ya truh-**zairm***
   Could you bring me...
2. *Bong dee-a. Kud-**zayzh**ang too-**mar**?*
   Good morning. What would you like?
3. *Oo p'**kennoo** al-**mohs**oo, fash fuh-**vor**.*
   Breakfast, please.

uma chávena de café *shavvna d'kaf-**fay*** a cup of Coffee	quente/frio *kent/**free**-oo* Hot/Cold	pão/papo-secos/torradas *powng/**paapoo say**koosh/to**raad**ush* Bread/Rolls/Toast
(com) leite *(kong) layt* (with) Milk	um chocolate *shookoo-**laat*** a Chocolate	manteiga/doce de laranja *mun**tayg**a/doss d'la-**ranzh**a* Butter/Marmalade

Restaurants – Booking a table

1. *Pawsoo r'zer-**var** ooma mayza purra **kwat**roo purra ush nawv?*
   Could I book a table for four at 9 o'clock?
2. *Oo **say**oo nawm, fash fuh-**vor**?*
   What's your name, please?

... or just turning up on spec

1. *Teng ooma mayza purra traysh, fash fuh-vor?*
    Have you a table for three, please?

2. *Oong moo-maintoo... oo s'n-yor r'zer-voh?*
    Just a moment... have you booked?

Ordering a meal

1. *Uh leeshta, s'fash fuh-vor.*
    The menu, please.

2. *Purra koom-sar – ooma sawpa dorta-leessa, ee d'polsh – oong beef kong buh-taatush freetush ee suh laada.*
    First – vegetable soup, and then – steak with chips/fries and salad.

3. *Oo kuh noosh ukkon-sailya purra oo muh-neenoo/uh muh-neena?*
    What do you suggest for the boy/girl?

4. *—, eng kuh kon-seest?*
    —, what's in it?

5. *D'zayzhang soobra-maiza?*
    Would you like dessert?

★ Tem pratos vegetarianos?

Teng praatoosh v'zha-turry-aanoosh?

Have you any vegetarian dishes?

20

15. *Tart dee uh-**men**doo-a*
    Almond tart

14. *Poo-**deeng** flang*
    Creme caramel

13. *Zh'**laad**oosh*
    Ice cream

13. *Buh-**taat**ush **freet**ush*
    Chips/Fries

12. *Fay-**zhowng** vaird*
    Green beans

11. *Suh-**laad**a meeshta oh roossa*
    Mixed or Russian salad

10. ***Treep**ush a mawda doo **Port**oo*
    Tripe Oporto-style

9. ***Frang**oo uh-**saad**oo*
    Roast chicken

— *Lista* —

Entradas e Sopas – Starters
1. Canja de Galinha
2. Pasta de fígado

Peixe – Fish
3. Caldeirada
4. Filetes de pescada
5. Bacalhau à Gomes de Sá

Carne – Meat
6. Cozido à portuguesa
7. Costeletas de carneiro
8. Carne de vaca assada
9. Frango assado
10. Tripas à moda do Porto

Legumes e saladas – Vegetables & salads
11. Salada mixta ou russa
12. Feijão verde
13. Batatas fritas

Sobremesa – Dessert
14. Gelados
15. Pudim flan
16. Tarte de amêndoa

Prato do dia – Today's special

Dishes usually come with rice/potatoes and vegetables

8. *Karn d'vakka uh-**saad**a*
   Roast beef

1. ***Kanzh**a d'guh-**leen**ya*
   Chicken broth

2. *Paashta d'**feeg**a-doo*
   Liver pâté

3. *Kalday-**raad**a*
   Fish stew

4. *Fee-**letsh** dupp'sh-**kaad**a*
   Hake fillets in batter

5. *Bukkul-**yow** a Gawmsh d'Sá*
   Salt Cod, onions, olives, boiled eggs

6. *Koo-**zeed**oo a poortoo-**gayz**a*
   Meat, sausage & vegetable stew

7. *Koosht-**lett**ush d'kur-**nay**roo*
   Lamb chops

Gelados/Sorvetes – Zh'laadoosh – Ice cream

Ananás
*unna-**nash***
Pineapple

Baunilha
*bow-**neel**ya*
Vanilla

Morango
*moo-**rang**oo*
Strawberry

Nata
naata
Cream

Pistáchio
*peesh-**tash**yoo*
Pistachio

1. *Teng zh'**laad**oosh?*
   Have you any ice cream?
3. *Oong d'shookoo-**laat**, s'fash fuh-**vor***.
   A chocolate one, please.
2. *Sing, **tain**yoo d'shookoo-**laat**, unna-**nash** ee moo-**rang**oo.*
   Yes, I've got chocolate, pineapple and strawberry.
4. *Grand oh p'**kenn**oo?*
   Large or small?

Self-service/Choosing things

1. *Esht, fash fuh-**vor**.*
   This, please.
2. *Oong **days**ush.*
   One of those.
3. *Kong luh-**goom**ush?*
   Which vegetables?
4. ***Esht**ush ee uh-**kail**sh.*
   These and those.
5. ***Kaw**moo s'**shamma** **eesht**oo?*
   What's this called?

22 Ordering drinks — *a carta de vinhos* – the wine list

1. *Purra b'bair?*
   What would you like to drink?
2. *Ooma guh-raafa d'veenyoo teentoo (brangkoo, ro-zay), ee oong kalleess d'veenyoo doo portoo.*
   A bottle of red wine (white, *rosé), and a glass of port, please.   *Br. rosado
3. *Duh kaaza, duh ruh-zhowng?*
   House wine, local wine?
4. *Sing, duh kaaza – ee ooma aggwa meen-raal.*
   Yes, house wine – and some mineral water, please.
5. *Kong gash oh seng gash?*
   Fizzy or still?

Vinho verde – **veen**yoo vaird
Dão – *downg*

Requests and paying

Cutlery, etc. p.13

1. *Olya – awtra kool-yair, s'fash fuh-vor.*
   Excuse me – another spoon, please.
2. *Poo-deeya truh-zair m-eyesh powng, fash fuh-vor?*
   Could I have some more bread, please?
3. *Shta beng?*
   Is it all right?
4. *Sing, mweentoo beng.*
   It's very good, thank you.
5. *Olya – uh kawnta, s'fash fuh-vor.*
   Could I have the bill, please?
6. *A uh-kee oong ayroo.*
   There's a mistake here.

Shopping

ABERTO – Open   *FECHADO/ENCERRADO* – Closed

Opening times: Usually 9am-12.30pm, 3pm-7pm, closed Saturday afternoons.
Small shops can be hard to identify. Ask for **uma loja (de alimentação)** *(ooma lawzha dee ully-menta-sowng)* – a (food) shop. A supermarket is **um supermercado** and **o mercado** is the market.

How to ask:

Tem (maçãs)?
teng muh-sangsh)?
Have you (any apples)?

Queria (maçãs)
kree-a (muh-sangsh)
I'd like some (apples)

Quanto é?
kwantoo ay?
How much is it?

Um kilo de (tomates)
oong keeloo d' (too-maatsh)
A kilo of (tomatoes)

Meio kilo
mayoo keeloo
Half a kilo – 1lb

Duzentas e cinquenta (gramas)
doozaintush ee singkwenta
250 (grammes) – ½lb

Um (Meio) litro
oong (mayoo) leetroo
One (Half a) litre

Cem (gramas)
seng (grummush)
100 (grammes) – 3½ oz

Um pouco de (queijo)
oong pawkoo d' (kayzhoo)
A little (cheese)

Uma fatia de (fiambre)
ooma fuh-teeya d' (fee-ambr)
A slice of (ham)

Quanto?
kwantoo?
How much/many?

Este/Um desses
esht/oong days'sh
This one/One of those

Um/uma, dois
oong/ooma, doish
One, two

Chega?
shayga?
Is that enough?

Um pouco mais/menos
oong pawkoo my-sh/maynoosh
A little more/less

Grande, pequeno/a
grand, p'kennoo/a
Big, small

Já chega
cha shayga
That's fine

Mais alguma coisa?
my-sh al-gooma koiza?
Anything else?

Estou só a ver
shtoo so uh vair
I'm just looking

Note: Use the conversation pattern shown in the baker's at all shops. Say **Bom dia** or **Boa tarde** – Good morning/afternoon – going in, and **Adeus, obrigado (obrigada** if you're a woman) – Goodbye, thank you – on leaving.

24 Padaria – *Padduh-reeya* – **Baker's**

1. *Bong dee-a.*
   Good morning.
3. *Teng powng? Oong **may**dee-o, fash fuh-**vor**. Esht.*
   Have you any bread?
   A medium-sized loaf, please.
   This one.

2. *Bong dee-a. Kud-**zayzh**a?*
   Good morning.
   What would you like?
4. *Oong powng grand oh oong powng p'**kenn**oo? Uh-**seeng**?*
   A big loaf or a little one?
   Like this?
5. *P'**kenn**oo.*
   A small one.   *Br. menor

1. *Ee maya **doozy**-a d'**paap**oo **say**koosh (kur-**kass**ush).*
   And half a dozen rolls.
3. *Nowng, ay **tood**oo, obry-**gaad**oo/a. **Kwan**too ay?*
   No, that's all, thank you.
   How much is it?

2. *Uh-**kee** i-**shta**. M-**eye**sh al-**goom**a koiza?*
   Here you are.
   Is that everything?
4. *Sowng — **shkood**oosh.*
   That's — escudos.
5. *Bong dee-a ee obry-**gaad**oo/a.*
   Thank you. Goodbye.

Grocer's – *Mercearia*
(in *English* order)

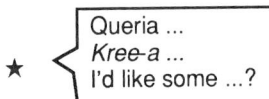
Queria ...
Kree-a ...
I'd like some ...?

Teng ... ?
Teng ... ?
Have you any ...?

CERVEJA
s'vayzha
Beer

BOLACHAS
boo-lashush
Biscuits/Cookies

MANTEIGA
mun-tayga
Butter

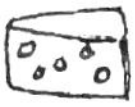

QUEIJO
kayzhoo
Cheese

CAFÉ
kaf-fay
Coffee

(meia dúzia de) OVOS
ohvoosh
(½ dozen) Eggs

SUMO de FRUTA
soomoo d'froota
Fruit Juice

DOCE
doss
Jam

MARGARINA
murga-reena
Margarine

LEITE (magro)
layt magroo
(skimmed) Milk

ÓLEO
awlyoo
Oil

MASSAS
massush
Pasta

ARROZ
uh-rawsh
Rice

DETERGENTE
d'ter-zhent
Soap Powder

AÇÚCAR
uh-sookar
Sugar

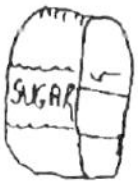

CHÁ
sha
Tea

PAPEL HIGIÉNICO
puh-pel
eezhy-ennykoo
Toilet Paper

LÍQUIDO para LAVAR A LOIÇA
leeky-doo purra luh-vaara loisa
Washing-up Liquid

AGUA MINERAL
aggwa meen-raal
Mineral Water

VINHO TINTO/
BRANCO
veenyoo teentoo/brangkoo
Red/White Wine

IOGURT
yoh-goort
Yogurt

SAL	PIMENTA	VINAGRE
sal	*pee-menta*	*vee-nagr*
Salt	Pepper	Vinegar

26 *Talho – tal-yoo – Butcher's   Carne – Meat
(in *Portuguese* order)   *Br. Açougue

Queria —
Kree-a —
I'd like some —

ASSADO
uh-saadoo
Roast

um BIFE
oong beef
a Steak

CABRITO
kuh-breetoo
Kid

CARNEIRO
kar-nayroo
Lamb

Carne de PORCO
karn d'porkoo
Pork

Carne de VACA
karn d'vakka
Beef

Carne de VITELA
karn d'vee-tayla
Veal

Carne PICADA
karn pee-kaada
Mince

COELHO
kwail-yo
Rabbit

COSTELETAS
koosht-laytush
Chops/Cutlets

ENTRECOSTO
entr'kawshtoo
Rib

FÍGADO
feega-doo
Liver

FRANGO
frangoo
Chicken

LOMBO
lomboo
Fillet

um PATO
oong paatoo
a Duck

RINS
reengsh
Kidneys

TRIPA
treepa
Tripe

Cold meat/Delicatessen – *Charcutaria*

CHOURIÇO
sho-reessoo
spicy Pork Sausage

CHOURIÇO DE SANGUE
sho-reessoo d'sang
Black Pudding

um EMPADÃO
empa-downg
a large Pie

FIAMBRE
fee-ambr
boiled Ham

MORTADELA
moorta-dayla
Salami

PRESUNTO
pruh-zoontoo
smoked Ham

SALSICHAS
sal-seeshush
Sausages

Fish – Seafood

(in *Portuguese* order)

Peixe
paysh
Fish

AMÊIJOAS
*um-**mayzh**oo-ush*
Clams

ATUM
*uh-**toong***
Tuna

BACALHAU
*bukkul-**yow***
Cod

ESPADARTE
*shpa-**dart***
Swordfish

GAMBAS
***gamb**ush*
Prawns

Mariscos
*muh-**reesh**koosh*
Seafood

MEXILHÕES
*m'sheel-**yoingsh***
Mussels

PESCADA
*p'sh-**kaad**a*
Hake

PEIXE ESPADA
*paysh ish-**paad**a*
Scabbard fish

SALMONETES
*sal-mo**naytsh***
red Mullet

SARDINHAS
*sur-**deen**yush*
Sardines

uma LAGOSTA
*ooma luh-**gosh**ta*
a Lobster

LINGUADO
*leeng-**waad**oo*
Sole

LULAS
***lool**ush*
Squid

uma TRUTA
ooma troota
a Trout

WEIGHTS AND MEASURES

5km = 8mls

DRY WEIGHTS   LIQUID MEASURES

1lb. = 454g.   1kg. = 2lb. 3oz.   1litre = U.S. 2 pts. 1 1/2 fl.oz. = 1 3/4 Imp. pts.

28 Vegetables – Legumes *(luh-goomush)*
(in *English* order)

Um kilo de...
oong keeloo d'...
A kilo of... ★

um PEPINO
oong pay-peenoo
a Cucumber

ALHO
al-yoo
Garlic

AZEITONAS
uzzay-tawnush
Olives

CEBOLAS
s'bolush
Onions

ALCACHOFRAS
alka-shofrush
Artichokes

ESPARGOS
***shparg**oosh*
Asparagus

BERINGELAS
*breen-**zhail**ush*
Aubergines

ABACATES
*ubba-**caats***
Avocados

FAVAS
***faav**ush*
Broad Beans

FEIJÃO VERDE
*fay-**zhowng** vaird*
Green Beans

COUVE/REPOLHO
*kawv/ray-**pol**yoo*
Cabbage

CENOURAS
*say-**nor**ush*
Carrots

AIPO
***eye**-poo*
Celery

GRÃO
*gr-**owng***
Chickpeas

MILHO
***meel**yoo*
Corn

LENTILHAS
*lain-**teel**yush*
Lentils

uma ALFACE
*ooma al-**fass***
a Lettuce

COGUMELOS
*koogoo-**mail**oosh*
Mushrooms

ERVILHAS
*eer-**veel**yush*
Peas

um PIMENTO
*oong pee-**main**too*
a Green Pepper

BATATAS
*buh-**taat**ush*
Potatoes

Fruit & Vegetables

Queria...
kree-a...
I'd like some...

um SACO
*oong **sakk**oo*
a Bag

Fruit – Fruta *(froota)*

AMÊNDOAS
ummaindoo-ush
Almonds

MAÇÃS
muh-sangsh
Apples

ALPERCHES
al-pairshush
Apricots

BANANAS
buh-naanush
Bananas

uma TORANJA
ooma too-ranzha
a Grapefruit

UVAS
oovush
Grapes

um LIMÃO
oong lee-mowng
a Lemon

um MELÃO
oong m'lowng
a Melon

NOZES
nawzush
Nuts

LARANJAS
luh-ranzhush
Oranges

PÊSSEGOS
paysa-goosh
Peaches

PERAS
payrush
Pears

um ANANÁS
oong unna-nash
a Pineapple

AMEIXAS
uh-mayshush
Plums

Tem...?
teng...?
Have you any...?

ESPINAFRES
shpee-naafrush
Spinach

TOMATES
oo-maatush
Tomatoes

CEREJAS
say-rayzhush
Cherries

FIGOS
feegoosh
Figs

MORANGOS
moo-rangoosh
Strawberries

uma MELANCIA
ooma m'lansee-a
a Water-melon

30 Toiletries and Medicines

> Queria —
> *Kree*-a —
> I'd like — ★

LOÇÃO ANTISÉPTICA
loos-owng anti-sayteeka
Antiseptic Cream

CHAMPÔ
shum-poh
Shampoo

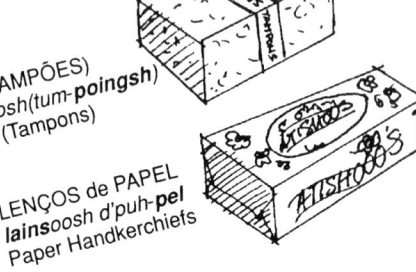

ASPIRINA
ushpi-reena
some Aspirin

ALGODÃO
algoo-downg
some Cottonwool

PENSOS HIGIÉNICOS (TAMPÕES)
pensoosh eezhy-ennykoosh (tum-poingsh)
Sanitary Napkins/Towels (Tampons)

LENÇOS de PAPEL
lainsoosh d'puh-pel
Paper Handkerchiefs

CONDÕES
kon-doingsh
Condoms

uma LIGADURA
ooma leega-doora
a Bandage

ADESIVOS
ud-seevoosh
Plasters/Band-Aid

uma GILETTE
ooma zhe-lait
a Razor

ALIMENTOS INFANTIS
alli-maintoosh infan-teesh
some Baby Food

LOÇÃO contra INSECTOS
loo-sowng kawntra in-saytoosh
Insect Repellant

SABONETE
subboo-nait
some Soap

FRALDAS
fraldush
Nappies/Diapers

ÓCULOS de SOL
awkooloosh d'sol
some Sunglasses

PASTA de DENTES
pashta d'dengtsh
Toothpaste

uma ESCOVA de DENTES
ooma shkova d'dengtsh
a Toothbrush

um PENTE
oong paint
a Comb

um DESODORIZANTE
dezo-doory-zant
a Deodorant

ÓLEO BRONZEADOR
awlyoo brawnzeeya-do
Suntan Cream

Onde posso comprar? Where can I get?

awnd pawsoo komprar?

Livraria	Papelaria	Quiosque
Bookshop	Stationery	Newsagent

um DICIONÁRIO
oong deesyoo-naary-oo
a Dictionary

(português-inglês)
(poortoo-gaysh eeng-laysh)
(Portuguese-English)

um JORNAL (inglês)
oong zhoor-naal (eeng laysh)
an (English) Newspaper

um LIVRO
oong leevroo
a Book

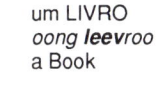

uma PLANTA (MAPA)
ooma planta (mappa)
a street (road) Map

um ROLO de FILME
oong rawloo d'feelm
a Film

uma BIC
ooma beek
a Biro

um LAPIS
oong laapsh
a Pencil

TABACARIA	FERRAGENS
Tobacconist's	Hardware

um SELO
oong sailoo
a Stamp

um POSTAL/Postais
poosh-taal/-t-eye-sh
a Postcard/Postcards

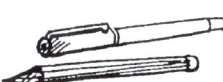

um ABRE-LATAS
oong abbr'/aatush
a Tin/Can Opener

uma BOTIJA de GÁS
boo-teezha d'gash
a Gas Cylinder

FÓSFOROS
fawshfoo-roosh
Matches

um ISQUEIRO
oong eesh-kayroo
a Lighter

uma LAMPADA
de ALGIBEIRA
*lampa-da dee
alzhee-bayra*
a Torch/Flashlight

CIGARROS
see-garroosh
Cigarettes
(com filtro)
(with filter)

uma AGULHA e LINHA
ooma uh goolya ee leenya
a Needle and Thread

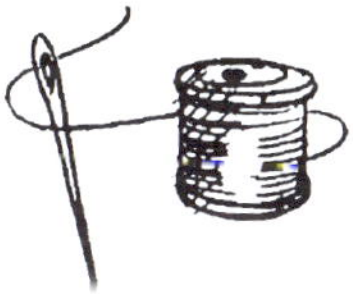

uma PILHA
ooma peel-ya
a Battery

um SACA-ROLHAS
oong sakka rawl-yush
a Corkscrew

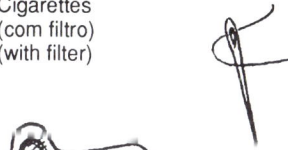

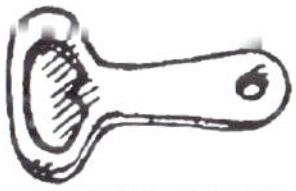

um ABRE-GARRAFAS
oong abbr'gur-raffush
a Bottle Opener

CORDA
korda
String, Rope

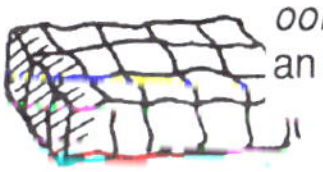

uma TESOURA
ooma t'zora
some Scissors

uma PLACA de GELO
ooma plakka d'zhailoo
an Ice Pack

32 Buying clothes (Colours/Colors: front cover)

1. *Bong dee-a. Kree-a ooma blooza.*
   Good morning, I'd like a blouse.*

2. *Kwaal **ay** oo **say**oo tuh-**mun**yoo?*
   What size do you take?

   *individual items p.34

3. *Ay oo kwuh-**ren**ta. Mush pod tee-**rar** uh meenya m'**deed**a?*
   I take size 40. But could you measure me?

4. *Teng al-**goom**a koiza eng uh-**zool**?*
   Have you anything in blue?

A Farmácia – *uh fur-massy-a* – the Chemist/Drugstore

Medicines are only sold at the *Farmácia,* usually open 9am-1pm, 3pm-7pm.
Buy toiletries at the *Drogaria* (p.30).
Farmácia de Serviço – Duty chemist.   *Aberta toda a noite* – Open all night

Tem alguma coisa para...?	a tosse	a diarreia
*Teng al-**goom**a koiza purra...*	*uh tawss*	*uh deeya-**ray**a*
Have you anything for — ?	a Cough	Diarrhoea

a prisão de ventre	a dor de cabeça	o enjoo do mar
*pree-**zowng** d'vaintr*	*dor d'kuh-**bay**sa*	*ain-**zhoh**-oo doo mar*
Constipation	a Headache	Seasickness

a dor de ouvido	uma mordedura de insecto	a dor de estômago
*dor dee oh-**veed**oo*	*moorda-**door**a deen-**say**too*	*dor dush-**tohm**a-goo*
Earache	an Insect Bite	Stomach Ache

a febre de feno	uma dor de garganta	a queimadura de sol
*febbr d'**fay**noo*	*dor d'gur-**gan**ta*	*kayma-**door**a d'sol*
Hay Fever	a Sore Throat	Sunburn

(*See also* Medical section p.57, Parts of the body p.60)]

1. **Paw**soo praw-**var**?
   Can I try it on?
2. Shta **beng**.
   It's fine.
3. Em-**ween**too grand/p'**kenn**oo.
   It's too big/small.
4. Nowng m'**feek**a beng.
   It doesn't fit me.
5. Em-**ween**too **kaar**oo.
   It's very dear.

Methods of payment

1. **Gawsh**too desht. Kree-a lay-**va** loo. **Kwan**too kooshta?
   I like this one. I'll take it. How much is it?
2. Poo-**dee**ya puh-**gar** nuh k-**eye**sha?
   Please pay at the cash desk.
5. D'**nadd**a.
   Not at all.
3. Uh-**say**tang kur-**toings**h d'**kraid**y-too/ay-ooro-**shaiksh**/ dollersh/shaiksh d'vee-**aazh**eng?
   Do you take credit cards/ Eurocheques/dollars/traveller's cheques?
4. **Mween**too obry-**gaad**oo/a.
   Thank you very much.

34 Roupa – *Ropa* – **Clothes**

de Senhora/Homem/Criança
Ladies', Men's, Children's

um CHAPÉU
*oong shuh-**pay**oo*
a Hat

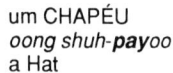

uma CAMISA/BLUSA
*ooma kuh-**meez**a/blooza*
a Shirt/Blouse

um *FATO de BANHO (Br. maiô)
*oong **faat**oo d'**bun**yoo*
a Swimming Costume

umas CUECAS
*oomush **kway**kush*
Underpants/Briefs

um VESTIDO
*oong v'sh-**teed**oo*
a Dress

uns CALÇÕES
*oongsh kal-**soingsh***
some Shorts

umas CALÇAS
*oomush **kals**ush*
some Trousers

uma SAIA
*ooma s-**eye**-a*
a Skirt

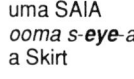

umas MEIAS
*oomush **may**ush*
some Tights

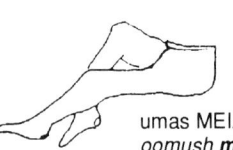

uma CAMISOLA
*ooma kummy-**zawl**a*
a Jumper

um CINTO
*oong **seen**too*
a Belt

umas PEÚGAS
*oomush pay-**oog**ush*
some Socks

uma GABARDINA
*ooma gubbar-**deen**a*
a Raincoat

uns SAPATOS
*oongsh suh-**paat**oosh*
some Shoes

umas SANDÁLIAS
*oomush sun-**daal**yush*
some Sandals

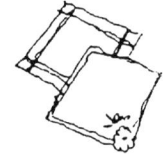

um LENÇO
*oong **lains**oo*
a Handkerchief

umas LUVAS
*oomush **loov**ush*
some Gloves

Banks

Hours:

Portugal
Monday to Friday
8.30am-2.45pm

Brazil
Monday to Friday
10am-4.30pm

Public holidays – *Feriados*

New Year's Day	January 1	*Ano Novo*	P/B
Shrove Tuesday	March	*Terça-feira de Carnaval*	P/B
Good Friday	March/April	*Sexta-feira Santa*	P/B
Tiradentes' Day	April 21	*Tiradentes*	B
Liberation Day	April 25	*o Vinte e cinco de Abril*	P
May Day	May 1	*Dia de Trabalho*	P/B
Corpus Christi	early June	*Corpo de Deus*	P/B
National Day	June 10	*Dia de Portugal*	P
Assumption	August 15	*Dia de Assunção*	P
Independence Day	September 7	*Independência*	B
Republic Day	October 5	*Proclamação da República*	P
Patron Saint's Day	October 12	*Nossa Senhora da Aparecida*	B
All Saints' Day	November 1	*Todos os Santos*	P
All Souls' Day	November 2	*Finados*	B
Republic Day	November 15	*Proclamação da República*	B
Independence Day	December 1	*Restauração da Independência*	P
Imm. Conception	December 8	*Imaculada Conceição*	P/B
Christmas Day	December 25	*Dia de Natal*	P/B

36 Bank, Exchange: *Banco, Câmbio*

1. *Olya, fash fuh-vor, awnd a uh-kee oong bangkoo?*
   Excuse me please, where is the nearest bank?
2. *A uh-lee oong, nuh prassa.*
   There's one over there, in the square.

Currency: P. o escudo ($)   dólares   libras   dinheiro
um conto = 1000 escudos   ***dollersh***   ***leeb****rush*   *deen**yay**roo*
Br. o real   dollars   £   money

1. *Kree-a trawkar deen-yayroo, oong ayooro-shaik/shaik d'vee-aazheng.*
   I'd like to change some money, a Eurocheque/traveller's cheque.
2. *Oo sayoo passa-port, fash fuh-vor.*
   Your passport, please.
3. *Uh-seen uh-kee, s'fash fuh-vor.*
   Sign here, please.
4. *Poo-deeya eer a k-eyesha.*
   Please collect it from the cashier.

Post Office – *Correios/CTT*

Open Monday to Friday 9am – 6pm.

Faz favor, onde é o correio?

*Fash fuh-**vor**, awndy-**ay** oo koo-**ray**oo?*

Where is the post office, please?

Buying stamps – *Selos*

1. Um selo, se faz favor. Para o Reino Unido/os Estados Unidos.
2. Para cartas ou postais?
3. Para postais.
4. São cem escudos (100$00).

Stamps sold here

1. *Oong **sai**loo, s'fash fuh-**vor**. Purra oo **Rain**oo Oo-**need**oo/oosh **Shtaad**oosh Oo-**need**oosh.*
   One stamp, please. To the U.K./U.S.A.
2. *Purra **kart**ush oh poosht-**eye**-sh?*
   For letters or postcards?
3. *Purra poosht-**eye**-sh.*
   Postcards.
4. *Sowng seng **shkood**oosh.*
   That will be 100 escudos.

38 The telephone – *o Telefone*

Onde há um telefone? ✱

*Awndy **a** oong t'lay-**fohn**?*
Where is there a phone?

Posso telefonar daqui? ✱

*Pawsoo t'layfon-**ar** duh-**kee**?*
Can I phone from here?

Emergency: 115 in Portugal (free). In Brazil each state has a different number. See front of telephone directory: *Pronto-socorro* – Accidents, *Bombeiros* – Fire Brigade, *Polícia* – Police.

Credifones use a phonecard *(um cartão)*, obtainable from post offices.
In Brazil use a token *(uma ficha)*.

International calls: in Portugal from a coin box or at the post office. In Brazil go to a public phone office *(uma estação telefônica)*.

Ringing home:
Dial 00 then your country code, followed by the town code (omit its first 0).
Britain .... dial 00 then 44
U.S. & Canada ..... dial 00 then 1
Australia .... dial 00 then 61
New Zealand .... dial 00 then 64
Eire .... dial 00 then 353

---

3. *Está?
4. Queria falar com o Senhor/a Senhora —
5. Fala João.
1. Queria fazer uma chamada para Inglaterra.
2. Queria fazer uma chamada paga no destinatário.

Introduzir as moedas
Insert coins

Depositar uma ou mais fichas
Insert one or more tokens

A extensão —
Extension —, please

1. *Kree-a fuh-**zair** ooma shuh-**maad**a purra Eengla-**terr**a.*
   I'd like to ring England.
2. *Kree-a fuh-**zair** ooma shuh-**maad**a paaga noo dushteena-**taary**-oo.*
   I'd like to make a reverse charge (collect) call.
3. *Shta?*
   Hallo? *Br. Alô?
4. *Kree-a fuh-**lar** kong oo s'n-**yor**/uh s'n-**yora** —.*
   I'd like to speak to Mr/Mrs —
5. *Falla Zhoo-**owng**.*
   This is John speaking.

Finding the way

Onde é – ?
*Awndy-**ay** – ?*
Where is – ?

> 1. Olhe, se faz favor, onde é (o caminho para Sagres)?
>
> 2. Atravesse a rua e tome a primeira à direita.
>
> 3. Podia-me indicar no mapa?
>
> 4. É longe?

1. *Olya, s'fash fuh-**vor**, awndy-**ay** (oo kuh-**meen**yoo purra **Sag**rush)?*
    Excuse me please, where is (the road to Sagres)?

2. *Uttra-**vayss** uh roo-a ee tawm uh pree-**may**ra a dee-**ray**ta.*
    Cross the road and take the first right.

3. *Poo-**dee**ya meendy-**kar** noo mappa?*
    Could you show me on the map, please?

4. *Ay lawnzh?*
    Is it far?

Directions/Locations

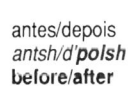

antes/depois
*antsh/d'**polsh***
before/after

ao lado de
*ow **lad**oo d'*
next to

aqui/ali
*uh-**kee**/uh-**lee***
here/there

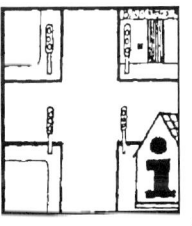

em frente de
ong fraint d'
opposite

na esquina
*nush-**kee**na*
on the corner

o cruzamento
*krooza-**main**too*
the crossroads

perto de
***pair**too d'*
near to

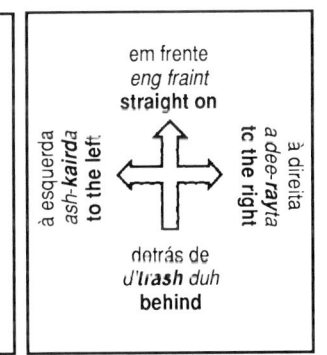

em frente
eng fraint
straight on

à esquerda
*ash-**kair**da*
to the left

à direita
*a dee-**ray**ta*
to the right

detrás de
*d'**trash** duh*
behind

Os Lavabos/
os Sanitários/o Toilete
*oosh luh-**vabb**oosh*
The Lavatory

Livre
leevra
Vacant

Homens
***aw**mengsh*
Gentlemen

Senhoras/Damas
*s'n-**yor**ush*
Ladies

W.C.

Ocupado
*ohkoo-**paa**doo*
Engaged

40 A Cidade – *uh see-daad* – **The Town**

a PRAIA
uh pr-eye-a
the Beach

a PONTE
uh pawnt
the Bridge

o CASTELO
oo kush-telloo
the Castle

a CATEDRAL
uh kuttay-draal
the Cathedral

a IGREJA
uh ee-grayzha
the Church

o CINEMA
oo see-naima
the Cinema

a BARRAGEM
uh buh-raazheng
the Dam

a QUINTA
uh keenta
the Farm, Estate

a COLINA
uh koo-leena
the Hill

o HOTEL
oo aw-tail
the Hotel

o MERCADO
oo mur-kaadoo
the Market

o MUSEU
oo moo-sayoo
the Museum

o PARQUE
oo park
the Park

a POLÍCIA
uh poo-leesy-a
the Police Station

o RIO
oo ree-oo
the River

41

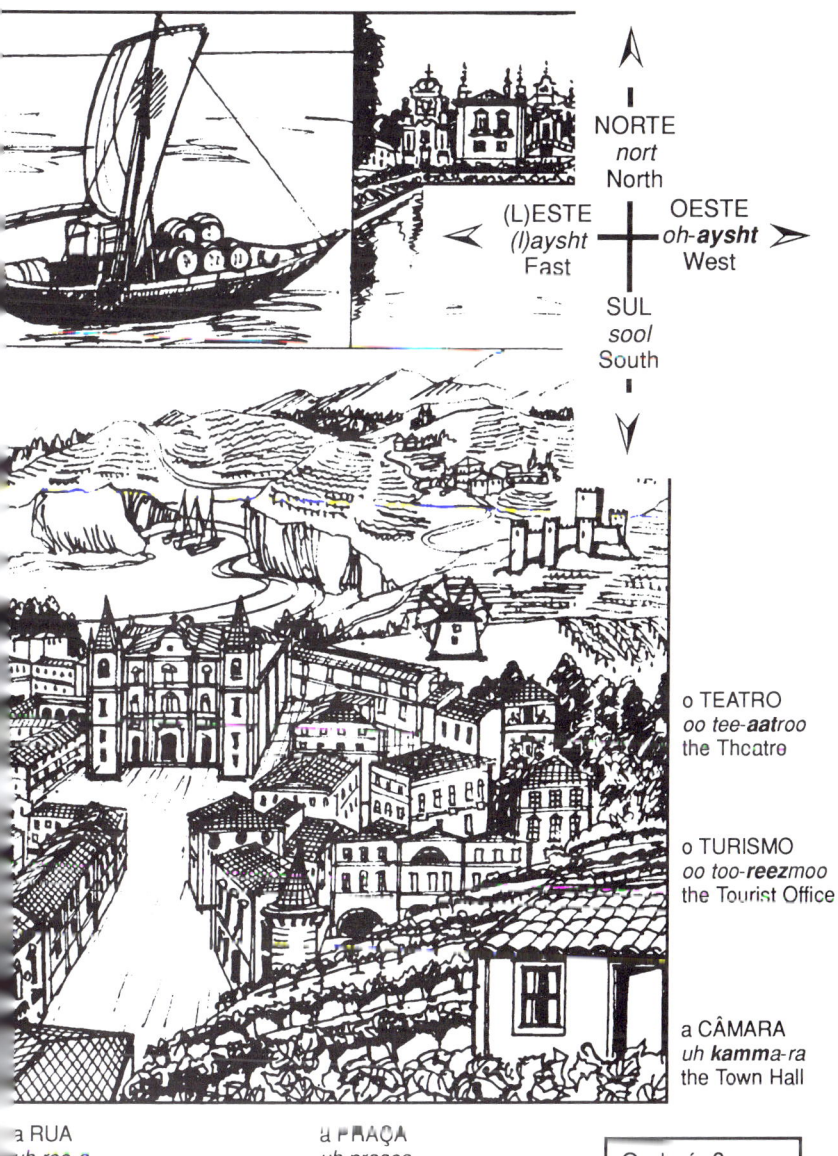

NORTE
nort
North

(L)ESTE
(l)aysht
East

OESTE
*oh-**aysht***
West

SUL
sool
South

o TEATRO
*oo tee-**aat**roo*
the Theatre

o TURISMO
*oo too-**reez**moo*
the Tourist Office

a CÂMARA
*uh **kamm**a-ra*
the Town Hall

a RUA
uh roo-a
the Road/Street

as LOJAS
*ush **lawzh**ush*
the Shops

a PRAÇA
uh praasa
the Square

a ESTAÇÃO
*ushta-**sowng***
the Station

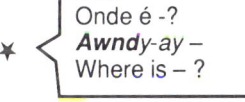

★ Onde é -?
Awndy-ay –
Where is – ?

Road travel

o carro/um táxi
*oo **kar**roo/**tax**ee*
the Car/Taxi

a bicicleta/motocicleta
*beesi-**klay**ta/**mo**tosi-**klay**ta*
the Bicycle/Motorcycle

*a praça de táxis
*uh prassa d'**tax**ees*
the Taxi Rank

*Br. o ponto de táxi

Boa viagem!
*boa vee-**aazh**eng*
Have a good trip!

Vou a pé
Vo uh pay
I walk

To park (or not...)

Parque de estacionamento - Car park

Instructions:
Moedas Utilizadas:
Takes these coins:

1. *Ocupar o lugar livre. Introduzir moedas até obter o tempo desejado.*
   Find space. Insert coins for time required.

2. *Premir o botão «bilhetes» para obtenção do mesmo.*
   Press «bilhetes» button to obtain ticket.

3. *Estacionamento pago todos os dias excepto domingos e feriados.*
   Fee payable except Sundays & holidays.

BILHETES Tickets

Botão de Anulação
Press to cancel

Além de 1/2 Hora

Over 1/2 hour

Estacionamento Pago/Tarifado

Paying zone

Tire o Bilhete no Parcómetro

Get ticket from meter

2ª à 6ª Feira

de Segunda à Sexta-Feira

Both mean Monday–Friday

Sábado/ aos Sábados

on Saturdays

Estacionamento proibido

Proibido estacionar

Both mean no parking

(nos) dias úteis

on weekdays

GRÁTIS Sab./Dom. e Feriados

FREE Sat./Sun. and holidays

Aut. Ligeiros

Light vehicles

On the open road
Atenção! - Take care!

Note: Traffic coming from the right has priority: *Dê prioridade* - Give way
Speed limits: 60km/37mph in towns, 90km/55mph in the country, 120km/75mph on motorways

Your right of way

No longer your right of way

Cruzamento perigoso
Dangerous X-roads

Inversão de marcha
U-turns allowed

Motor vehicles only

Proibido ultrapassar
No overtaking

Cuidado
Take care

Desvio
Diversion

(Fim de)
(End...)

Devagar
Slow

*Pare
Olhe
Escute*
Stop, look, listen

*Conduza
com cautela*
Drive carefully

Perigo
Danger

ALFÂNDEGA
ADUANA
Customs

Perigo de fogo!
No fires, matches, cigarettes, etc.

PEÃO
*NA ESTRADA
CAMINHE PELA
SUA ESQUERDA*
Pedestrians: walk on the left

Expressway/Motorway – Auto-estrada

PORTO
pela EN1

LISBOA PORTO A1
Portagem

PORTAGEM
Toll

Pela EN1
by EN1

Saída
Exit

trânsito local
Local traffic

Prepare pagamento
Get your money ready

Carregue aqui
Press here

Retire o título
Take ticket

Outras direcções
Other directions

área de serviço
Service area

Emergency: see pp 47 & 57
Look for orange emergency phone

Carregue no botão e aguarde o sinal de chamar
Press button and wait for answer.
(If no connection, use next SOS phone or ring **115**)

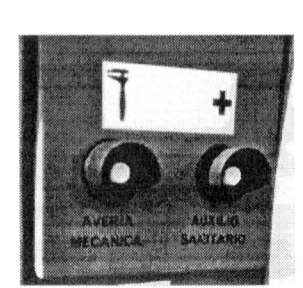

Averia Mecanica
Mechanical breakdown

Auxílio Sanitário
Medical assistance

Car hire – *Aluguer de carros/automóveis *Br. Aluguel   45

1. Bom dia, queria alugar um carro.
2. Que tipo de carro? Pequeno, grande, médio?

1. *Bong dee-a, kree-a ulloo-gar oong karroo.*
   Hallo, I'd like to hire a car.
2. *K'teepoo d'karroo? P'kennoo, grand, maidy-oo?*
   What sort of car – small, large, medium?

1. Para um dia? Para uma semana?
2. Qual é a tarifa?
3. Posso deixar o carro em Coimbra?
4. Está aqui a minha *carta de condução.

1. *Purra oong dee-a? Purra ooma s'maana?*
   For a day, a week?
2. *Kwaal-ay uh tuh-reefa?*
   What is the rate?
3. *Pawsoo day-shar oo karroo eng K'weembra?*
   Can I leave the car in Coimbra?
4. *Shta uh-kee uh meen-ya karta d'kondoo-sowng.*
   Here is my driving licence.

   *Br. *a carteira de motorista*

46 Gas/Petrol station – *Posto de gasolina, Estação de serviço*

> Desculpe, há uma estação de serviço aqui perto?

Gasolina		Gasóleo
guzzoo-leena		*gazzolly-oo*
Petrol/Gas		Diesel
Normal/Super		Álcool
nor-maal/soopair		*alkol*
2 star/4 star		Alcohol fuel (Br.)
Sem Chumbo		Mistura
seng shoomboo		*meesh-toora*
Unleaded		2-stroke mix
Ar	Óleo	Água
ar	*awlyoo*	*aggwa*
Air	Oil	Water

D'sh-koolp, a ooma shta-sowng d'sur-veesoo uh-kee pairtoo?
Excuse me, is there a filling station near here?

Aberto dia e noite/24 horas – Open day and night   *loja* – shop

> 1. Bom dia. Normal, super ou sem chumbo?
> 2. Sem chumbo. Encha o depósito, faz favor.
> 3. Faz favor, podia ver o óleo (a pressão das rodas)?
> 4. Quanto é?

1. *Bong dee-a. Nor-maal, soopair oh seng shoomboo?*
   Hallo. 2 star, 4 star or unleaded?
2. *Seng shoomboo. Ainsha oo d'pawzy-too, fash fuh-vor.*
   Unleaded. Fill it up, please.
3. *Fash fuh-vor, poo-deeya vair oo awlyoo (uh pruh-sowng dush rawdush)?*
   Could you check the oil (tyre pressure), please?
4. *Kwantoo ay?*
   How much is it?

Breakdowns and Repairs

1. Desculpe, tenho uma avaria.
2. Podia ajudar-me, faz favor?
3. Posso usar o vosso telefone, faz favor?
4. Onde fica a garagem mais perto?

1. *D'sh-**koolp**, **tain**yoo ooma uvva-**ree**ya.*
   Excuse me, I have broken down.
2. *Poo-**deey**a uzhoo-**darm**, fash fuh-**vor**?*
   Can you help me, please?
3. ***Paw**soo oo-**zar** oo **vaw**soo t'lay-**fohn**, fash fuh-**vor**?*
   Could I use your phone, please?
4. *Awnd feeka uh guh-**raazh**eng m-**eye**sh **pair**too?*
   Where is the nearest garage?

Emergency telephones and help: pp. 44 and 57.

Garagem de serviço/Reparações – Repairs

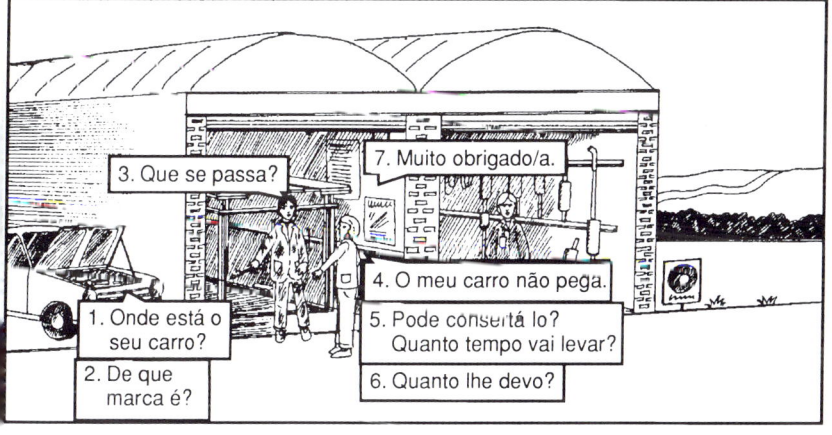

1. Onde está o seu carro?
2. De que marca é?
3. Que se passa?
4. O meu carro não pega.
5. Pode consertá-lo? Quanto tempo vai levar?
6. Quanto lhe devo?
7. Muito obrigado/a.

1. *Awnd shta oo **say**oo **kar**roo?*
   Where is your car now?
2. *D'kuh marka ay?*
   What make is it?
3. *Kuss passa?*
   What's the matter?
4. *Oo **may**oo **kar**roo nowng payga.*
   My car won't start.
5. *Pod konsair-**ta** loh? **Kwan**too taimpoo v-**eye** l'**var**?*
   Can you mend it? How long will it take?
6. ***Kwan**too l-**yuh** **day**voo?*
   What do I owe you?
7. *Mw**een**too obry-**gaa**doo/a.*
   Thanks very much.

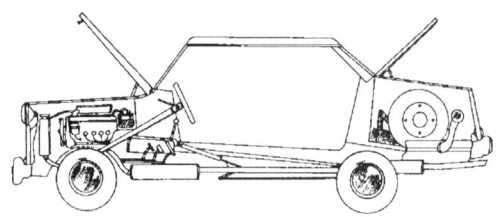

On two and four wheels

Preciso de um —
*Pruh-**seez**oo dee oong —*
I need a —

O — não funciona.
*Oo — nowng foons-**yawn**a.*
The — isn't working.

O motor para muitas vezes.
*Oo moh-**tor** purra **mween**tush **vayz**ush.*
The engine often stalls.

O motor está a aquecer muito.
*Oo moh-**tor** shta uh ukkay-**sair** **mween**too.*
The engine is overheating a lot.

Car, bicycle and motorcycle parts (in *English* order)

1. o FILTRO de AR
   *oo **feel**troo dee ar*
   the Air Filter

2. a BATERIA
   *uh **buttree**-a*
   the Battery

3. os TRAVÕES
   *oosh truh-**voingsh***
   the Brakes

4. uma LÂMPADA
   *ooma **lamp**a-da*
   a Bulb

5. o CABO do TRAVÃO
   *oo **kaab**oo doo truh-**vowng***
   the brake Cable

6. um BIDON de GASOLINA
   *oong bee-**dong** d'guzzoo-**leen**a*
   a gas/petrol Can

7. o CARBURADOR
   *oo kurboora-**dor***
   the Carburettor

8. a CADEIA
   *uh kuh-**day**a*
   the Chain

9. o BOTÃO de ARRANQUE
   *oo boo-**towng** duh-**rank***
   the Choke

10. a EMBREAGEM
    *uh **aimbree-aaz**heng*
    the Clutch

11. o DISTRIBUIDOR
    *oo dish-treebwee-**dor***
    the Distributor

12. o SISTEMA ELECTRICO
    *oo seesh-**tayma** eelettry-koo*
    the Electrical System

13. o MOTOR
    *oo moh-**tor***
    the Engine

14. o TUBO de ESCAPE
    *oo **toob**oo dish-**kap***
    the Exhaust

15. a CORREIA da VENTOÍNHA
    *uh koo-**ray**a duh vaintoo-**een**ya*
    the Fan Belt

16. um FUSO
    *oong **fooz**oo*
    a Fuse

17. uma JUNTA
    ooma zhoonta
    a Gasket

18. a CAIXA de VELOCIDADES
    *uh k-**eye**sha d'vullossy-**daad**ush*
    the Gearbox

19. as MUDANÇAS
    *ush moo-**dans**ush*
    the Gears

20. o GUIADOR
    *oo gheeya-**dor***
    the Handlebars (Bicycle)

21. os FARÓIS MÁXIMOS
    *oosh fuh-**roish** **massy**-moosh*
    the Headlights

22. o PISCA-PISCA
    oo peeshka peeshka
    the Indicator

23. uma CÂMARA de AR
    *ooma **kumma**-ra dee ar*
    an Inner Tube

24. a CHAVE de IGNIÇÃO
    *uh shaav dee eegny-**sowng***
    the Ignition Key

25. uma FUGA de ÓLEO/ÁGUA
    *ooma fooga dee **awl**y-oo/aggwa*
    an Oil/Water Leak

26. as LUZES
    *ush **looz**ush*
    the Lights

27. o PORTA-BAGAGEM
    *oo porta buh-**gaazh**eng*
    the Luggage Carrier

28. uma CORREIA para BAGAGEM
    *kor-**ray**a purra buh-**gaazh**eng*
    a Luggage Strap

29. o GUARDA-LAMAS
    *oo gwarda **lumm**ush*
    the Mudguard

30. uma PORCA de PARAFUSO
    *ooma porka d'purra-**foo**zoo*
    a Nut

31. os CONTACTOS
    *oosh kawn-**takt**oosh*
    the Points

32. a BOMBA
    uh bomba
    the Pump

33. o RADIADOR
    *oo ruddya-**dor***
    the Radiator

34. um SACO de SELIM
    *oong **sakk**oo duh suh-**leeng***
    a Saddlebag

35. um PARAFUSO
    *oong purra-**foo**zoo*
    a Screw, Bolt

36. uma CHAVE de PARAFUSOS
    *shaav duh purra-**foo**zoosh*
    a Screwdriver

37. o AMORTECEDOR
    *oo um**mortsa**-**dor***
    the Shock Absorber

38. o SILENCIADOR
    *oo see**lainsya**-**dor***
    the Silencer

39. uma CHAVE INGLESA
    *ooma shaav een-**glayza***
    a Spanner

40. uma VELA
    ooma vayla
    a Sparking Plug

41. os RAIOS (das Rodas)
    *oosh r-**eye**-oosh*
    the (Wheel) Spokes

42. uma CAIXA de FERRAMENTAS
    *ooma k-**eye**sha d'fra-**main**tush*
    a Tool Kit

43. um PNEU
    *oong p-**nay**oo*
    a Tyre

44. a PRESSÃO das RODAS
    *uh pruh-**sowng** dush **rawd**ush*
    the Tyre Pressure

45. uma VÁLVULA
    *ooma **valvoo**-la*
    a Valve

46. uma RODA
    ooma rawda
    a Wheel

47. o PÁRA-BRISAS
    *oo para **breez**ush*
    the Windscreen/-shield

48. um *LIMPA PÁRA-BRISAS
    *oong leempa para **breez**ush*
    a Windscreen Wiper
    *Br limpador de pára-brisas

Tenho um furo
***Tain**yoo oong **foo**roo*
I've got a Puncture/Flat

um CAPACETE
*oong kuppa-**sait***
a Crash Helmet

Bicicletas para alugar
Bicycles for hire

49

50 Rail travel

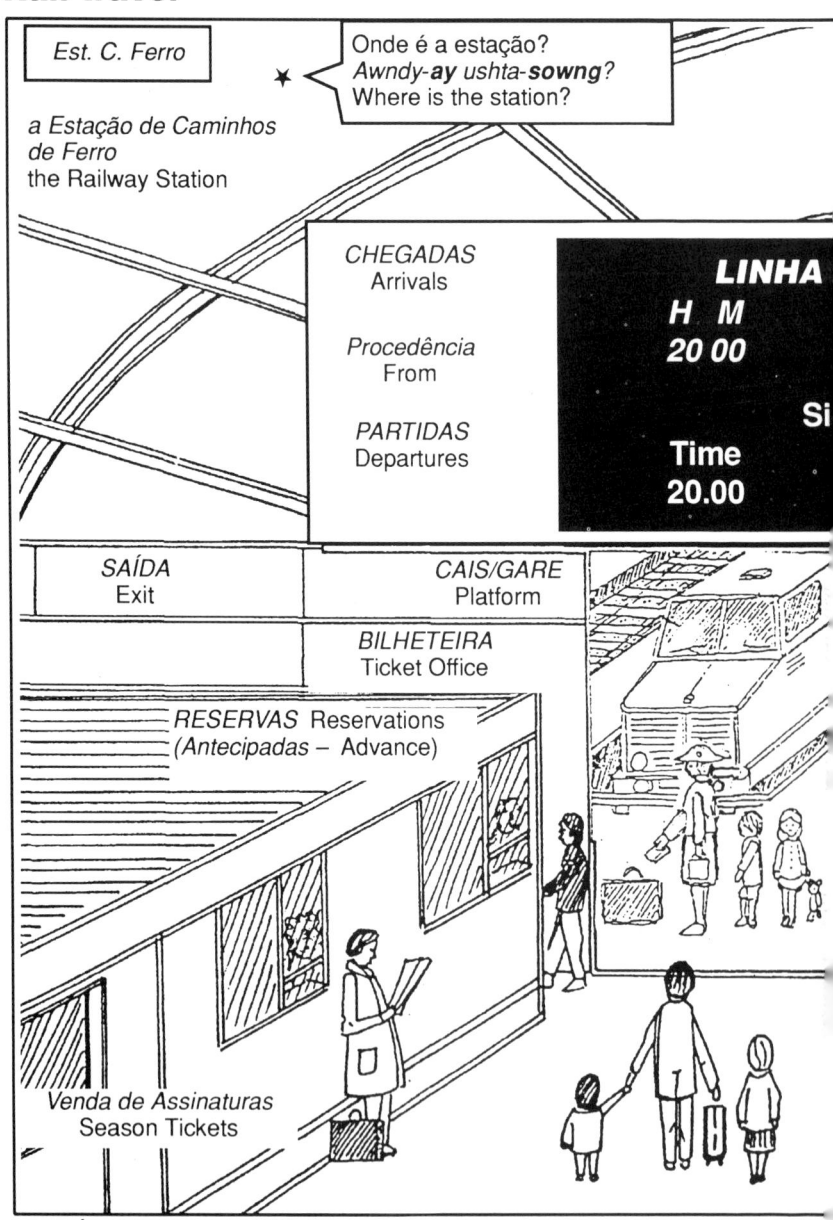

Est. C. Ferro

a Estação de Caminhos de Ferro
the Railway Station

Onde é a estação?
*Awndy-**ay** ushta-**sowng**?*
Where is the station?

CHEGADAS
Arrivals

Procedência
From

PARTIDAS
Departures

LINHA
H M
20 00

Si

Time
20.00

SAÍDA
Exit

CAIS/GARE
Platform

BILHETEIRA
Ticket Office

RESERVAS Reservations
(Antecipadas – Advance)

Venda de Assinaturas
Season Tickets

HORÁRIO: Timetable
de Ligação ao TGV para Paris:
connects with TGV to Paris

diário: daily
dias de semana: Monday to Saturday
domingos e feriados: Sundays & holidays
paragens: stops

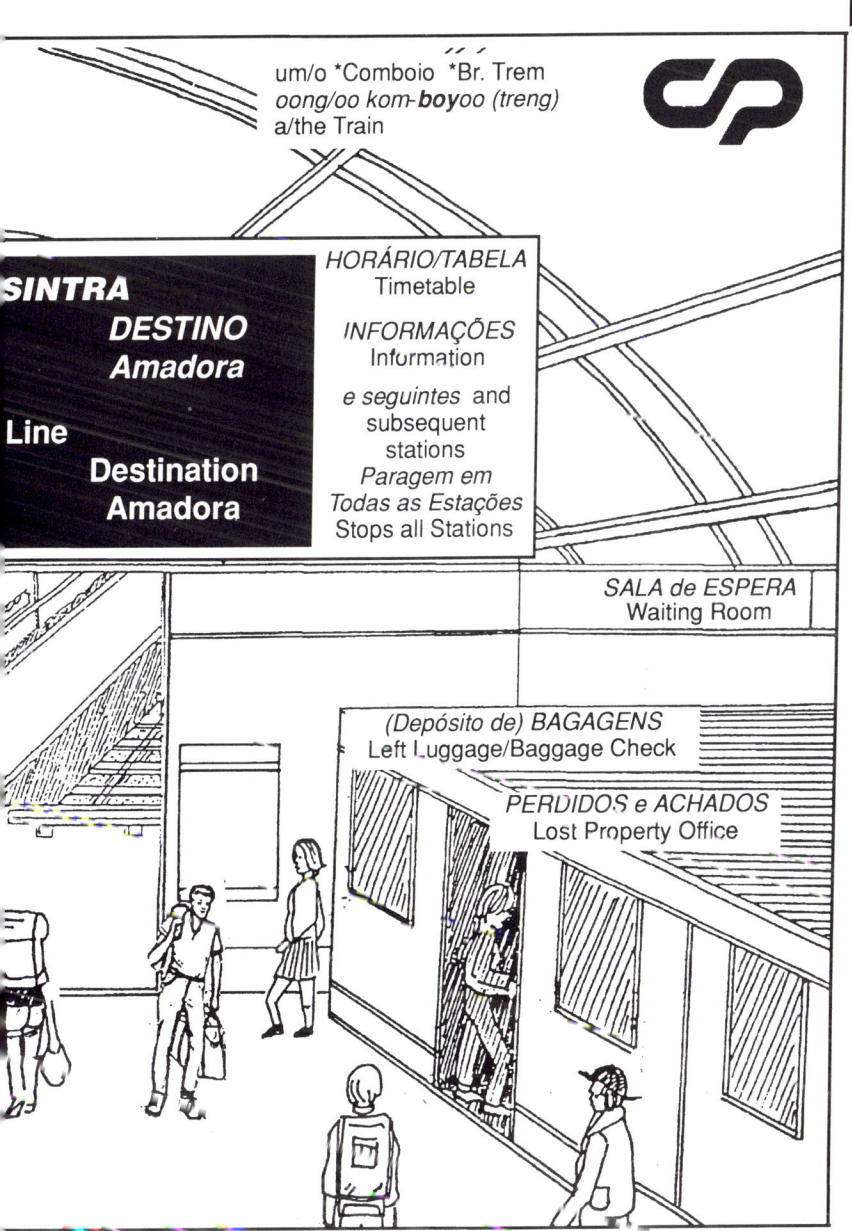

um/o *Comboio *Br. Trem
oong/oo kom-**boy**oo (treng)
a/the Train

SINTRA
DESTINO
Amadora

Line
Destination
Amadora

HORÁRIO/TABELA
Timetable

INFORMAÇÕES
Information

e seguintes and subsequent stations
Paragem em Todas as Estações
Stops all Stations

SALA de ESPERA
Waiting Room

(Depósito de) BAGAGENS
Left Luggage/Baggage Check

PERDIDOS e ACHADOS
Lost Property Office

Tipo de Comboio: Type of Train
Correio: Mail train; takes passengers
Intercidades: InterCity trains
Rápido: Direct train

52 Buying tickets: basic pattern

2. Quanto é?

1. Queria um *bilhete simples para o Porto, faz favor.

3. Queria reservar um lugar (beliche/cama).

Para Lisboa, faz favor
*Purra Leezh-**boa**, f.f.*
To Lisbon, please

Onde vai? – Vou...
*Awnd v-**eye**? – Voh...*
Where are you going?
I'm going...

Simples/de ida e volta
***seempl**sh/**deeda** ee **vawl**ta*
Single/Return (round trip)

Fumador ou não fumador?
*fooma-**dor** oh nowng fooma-**dor**?*
Smoker or Non-smoker

1. *Kree-a oong beel-**yet seempl**sh purra oo **Por**too, fash fuh-**vor**.*
   I'd like a single ticket to Oporto, please.

*Br. *uma passagem*

2. ***Kwan**too ay?*
   How much is it?

3. *Kree-a r'zer-**var** oong loo-**gar** (b'**leesh**/kumma).*
   I'd like to book a seat (couchette/sleeper).

---

1. *Fash fuh-**vor**, kwaal-**ay** uh gar purra oo Shtoo-**reel**?*
   Which is the platform for Estoril, please?

2. *Gar traysh.*
   Platform three.

3. *Uh kee **or**ush part oo kom-**boy**oo?*
   When does the train go?

Próxima Partida
Next Departure

N.B. You must have a ticket before boarding.

*Br. o trem *(treng)*

1. Faz favor, qual é a gare para o Estoril?

2. Gare três.

3. A que horas parte o *comboio?

Finding a seat

*1. Está ocupado?

2. Este é o *comboio para Coimbra?

*Br. trem

Não fumadores/
É proibido fumar
No smoking

*1. Shta ohkoo-**paad**oo?*
Is this seat taken?

Use this to ask for a seat anywhere.

2. *Eshty-**ay** oo kom-**boy**oo purra **Kweem**bra?*
Is this the train for Coimbra?

Local transport: o Metro – the Underground/Subway

Cancel ticket in machine on board Metro, trams or buses.

Um, faz favor.

1. Para o Saldanha – qual é a linha?

2. Preciso de mudar?

*Oong, fash fuh-**vor***
One, please.

1. *Purra oo Sul-**daan**ya – kwaal-**ay** uh leenya?*
For Saldanha – which line is it?

2. *Pruh-**seez**oo d'moo-**dar**?*
Do I have to change?

54 Buses and trams

Bus Stop
*Br. *Parada*

o autocarro (a camioneta)

the Bus (Intercity Bus)

*o *eléctrico*

the Tram
*Br. *o bonde*

1. A que horas parte a camioneta para Faro?
2. Donde parte a camioneta para Lagos?
3. Esta camioneta vai para Portimão?

1. *Uh kee **aw**rush part uh kamyoo-**nay**ta purra **Faa**roo?*
   When does the bus leave for Faro?

a *Gare Rodoviária/a estação de camionetas

the Bus Station   *Br. *estação rodoviária*

2. *Dawnd part uh kamyoo-**nay**ta purra **Laag**oosh?*
   Where does the bus for Lagos go from?

3. *Eshta kamyoo-**nay**ta v-**eye** purra Porty-**mowng**?*
   Does this bus go to Portimão?

1. Esta é a estação?
2. Desculpe, pode me dizer onde devo descer?

1. *Eshta-**ay** ushta-**sowng**?*
   Is this the station?

2. *D'sh-**koolp**, podm dee-**zair** awnd **day**voo d'sh-**sair**?*
   Excuse me, could you tell me where to get off?

Boats

Passeios de barco — Boat trips
Partidas cada 30 minutos — Departures every 30 minutes

É PERIGOSO / CUIDADO

Danger

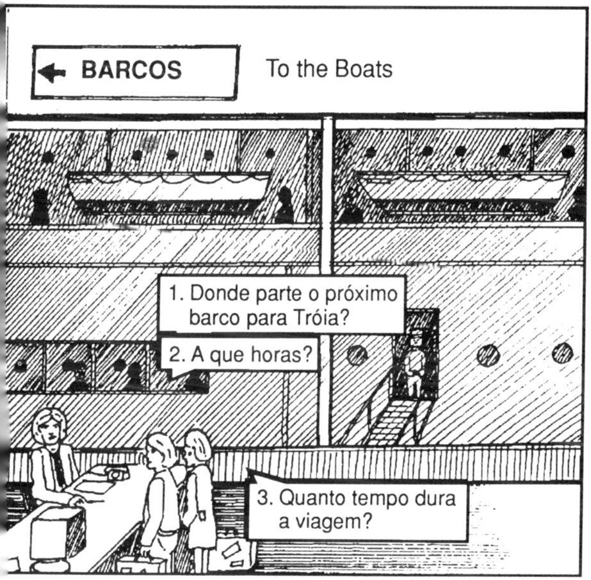

← BARCOS — To the Boats

no Porto
*noo **por**too*
at the Harbour

Aluguer de barcos

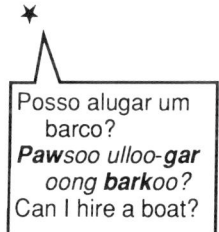

Boats for hire

1. Donde parte o próximo barco para Tróia?
2. A que horas?
3. Quanto tempo dura a viagem?

Posso alugar um barco?
***Paw**soo ulloo-**gar** oong **bar**koo?*
Can I hire a boat?

1. *Dawnd part oo **praws**y-moo **bar**koo purra **Traw**-ya?*
   Where does the boat to Tróia go from?
2. *Uh kee **awr**ush?*
   When?
3. ***Kwan**too **taim**poo doora uh vee-**aazh**eng?*
   How long does it take?

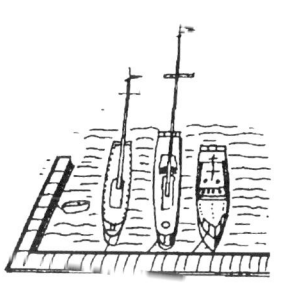

a Praia
*a pr-**eye**-a*
the Beach

a Canoa
*una kuh-**noh**-a*
Canoe/Rowing Boat

a Ilha
*a **eel**-ya*
the Island

o Lago
*oo **laag**oo*
the Lake

um Colete/Cinto de Salvação
*koo-**let**/**seen**too d'salva**sowng***
a Life Jacket/Belt

o Barco Salva-vidas
*oo **bar**koo salva-**veed**ush*
the Lifeboat

o Cais
*oo k-**eye**-sh*
the Pier

o Mar
oo mar
the Sea

um Barco à Vela
*oong **bar**koo a **vay**la*
a Yacht

a Marina
*uh muh-**reen**a*
the Yacht Harbour

56 Air travel

Como posso ir ao aeroporto?*
Kawmoo pawsoo eer ow uh-airo-portoo?
How do I get to the airport?

1. Quando é o próximo vôo para o Rio?
2. Às nove e dez.
3. É um vôo directo?
4. A que horas devo fazer o check-in?
5. Qual é o número do vôo?

o Avião
oo uvvy-owng
the Plane

Chegadas/Partidas
Arrivals/Departures...

domésticas/internacionais
...External/Internal

1. *Kwandoo-ay oo prawsy-moo voh-oo purra oo Ree-oo?*
   When is the next flight to Rio?

2. *Ash nawv ee desh.*
   At 9.10.

3. *Ay oong voh-oo dee-raytoo?*
   Is it a direct flight?

4. *Uh kee awrush dayvoo fuh-zair oo check-in?*
   What time is check in?

5. *Kwaal-ay oo noomroo doo voh-oo?*
   What is the flight number?

1. Queria mudar (cancelar) o meu bilhete.
2. Queria reservar um vôo para São Paulo na segunda-feira.

1. *Kree-a moo-dar (cansa-lar) oo mayoo beel-yet.*
   I'd like to change (confirm/cancel) my reservation.

2. *Kree-a r'zer-var oong voh-oo purra Sowng Pow-loo nuh s'goonda fayra.*
   I'd like to book a flight to São Paulo on Monday, please.

Accidents and illness

POSTO DE SOCORROS
PRONTO-SOCORRO
First Aid Post

✚ *CRUZ VERMELHA*
Red Cross

✚ *AMBULÂNCIA* ✚
Ambulance

URGÊNCIAS/
EMERGÊNCIA
Emergencies/
Casualty

HOSPITAL
Hospital

Emergency services: Ring **115** or see front cover of telephone book
Minor ailments: see Pharmacy section p.32

1. Socorro!
2. Venham depressa! Chame uma ambulância faz favor.

1. *So-**korr**ool*
   Help!

2. *Vainyang d'**prays**a! Sham ooma amboo-**langs**y-a fash fuh-**vor**.*
   Quick! Call an ambulance, please.

Calling the doctor/making an appointment

1. Estou doente. Preciso de um médico.
2. Queria ver o médico. Quando pode ser? É urgente.

Médico
Doctor

Centro da Saúde
Health Centre

Urgência Médica/
Atendimento Médico
Emergencies/Dr on duty

Horário...
Consulting hours...

Todos os dias/2ª a 6ª Feira
Daily/Monday to Friday

1. *Shto doo-**ent**. Pruh-**seez**oo dee oong **medd**y-koo.*
   I'm ill. I need a doctor.

2. *Kree-a vair oo **medd**y-koo. **Kwan**doo pod sair? Ay oor-**zhent**.*
   I'd like to see the doctor. When can I come? It's urgent.

58 At the doctor's (parts of the body page 60)

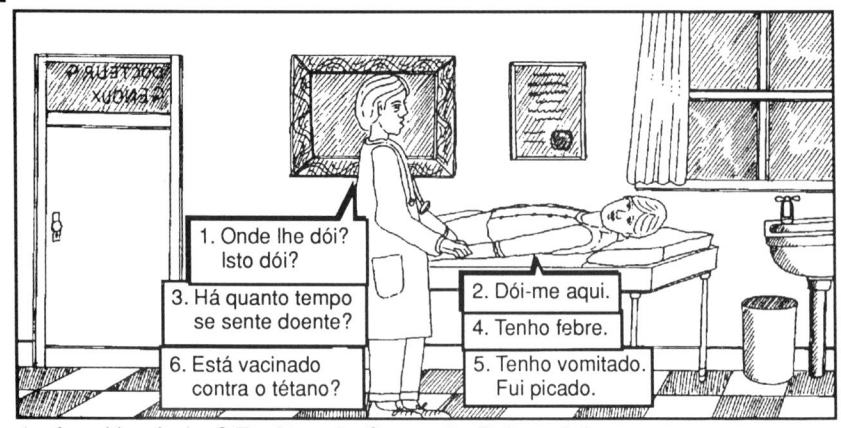

Speech bubbles (first scene):
1. Onde lhe dói? Isto dói?
2. Dói-me aqui.
3. Há quanto tempo se sente doente?
4. Tenho febre.
5. Tenho vomitado. Fui picado.
6. Está vacinado contra o tétano?

1. *Awnd l-yuh doy? Eeshtoo doy?*
   Where does it hurt? Does this hurt?
3. ***A kwan**too **taim**poo s'saint doo-**ent**?*
   How long have you been ill?
6. *Shta vussy-**naad**oo kawntra oo **tett**a-noo?*
   Have you been vaccinated against tetanus?
2. *Doima uh-**kee**.*
   It hurts here.
4. *Tainyoo febbr.*
   I have a temperature.
5. *Tainyoo voomy-**taad**oo. **Foo**-ee pee-**kaad**oo.*
   I've been sick. I've been stung.

Speech bubbles (second scene):
1. Estou a tomar estes medicamentos.
2. Podia dar-me uma receita?
3. Não deve comer... (beber)
4. For a child: Quantos anos tem?
5. Tem cinco anos.
6. Quanto lhe devo?

1. *Shto uh too-**mar** eshtush m'deeka-**maint**oosh.*
   I've been taking these medicines.
2. *Poo-**deey**a darm ooma r'**sayt**a?*
   Could you give me a prescription, please?
3. *Nowng dayv koo-**mair**... (b'**bair**)*
   You must not eat... (drink)
4. *Kwan**toosh unn**oosh teng?*
   How old is he/she?
5. *Teng **seengk**oo unn**oosh**.*
   He/she is five.
6. *Kwantoo l-yuh dayvoo?*
   How much do I owe you?

When to take your medicine:	**What the doctor needs to know:**
... *vezes por dia* ... times a day	*Sou...* alérgico/a* contra penicilina
	*So ... uh-**lairzhy**-koo/a kawntra*
	*p'neesee-**leen**a*
... *cada — horas* every — hours	I'm... allergic to penicillin
antes/depois de cada refeição	asmático/a* diabético/a*
before/after each meal	*azh-**maaty**-koo/a deeya-**betty**-koo/a*
	Asthmatic Diabetic
durante — dias for — days	epiléptico/a* Estou grávida
	*aypee-**letty**-koo/a shto **graavi**-da*
de manhã/de noite	Epileptic I'm Pregnant
in the morning/at night	
37°C = 98.6°F	*Sofro do coração*
	*sofroo doo koora-**sowng***
	I have Heart Trouble
*alérgico, etc. for men	
alérgica, etc. for women	*Tenho a tensão alta*
	*tainyoo uh teng-**sowng** alta*
	I have High Blood Pressure

At the Dentist –
Dentista/Médico Dentista

Consultas a partir da 1 da tarde
Surgery from 1 p.m.

1. *Tenho dor de dentes.*

2. *Queria marcar uma consulta para ver o dentista. É urgente.*

3. *Isto dói-lhe?*

4. *Dói-me aqui.*

1. ***Tainyoo** dor d'**dengt**sh.*
   I've got toothache.
2. *Kree-a mur-**kar** ooma kon-**sool**ta purra vair oo dain-**teesh**ta. Ay oor-**zhent**.*
   I'd like to make an appointment with the dentist. It's urgent.
3. *Ishton **doil**-ya?*
   Does that hurt?
4. *Doim uh-**koe***
   It hurts here.

60 **Parts of the body** – in *English* order

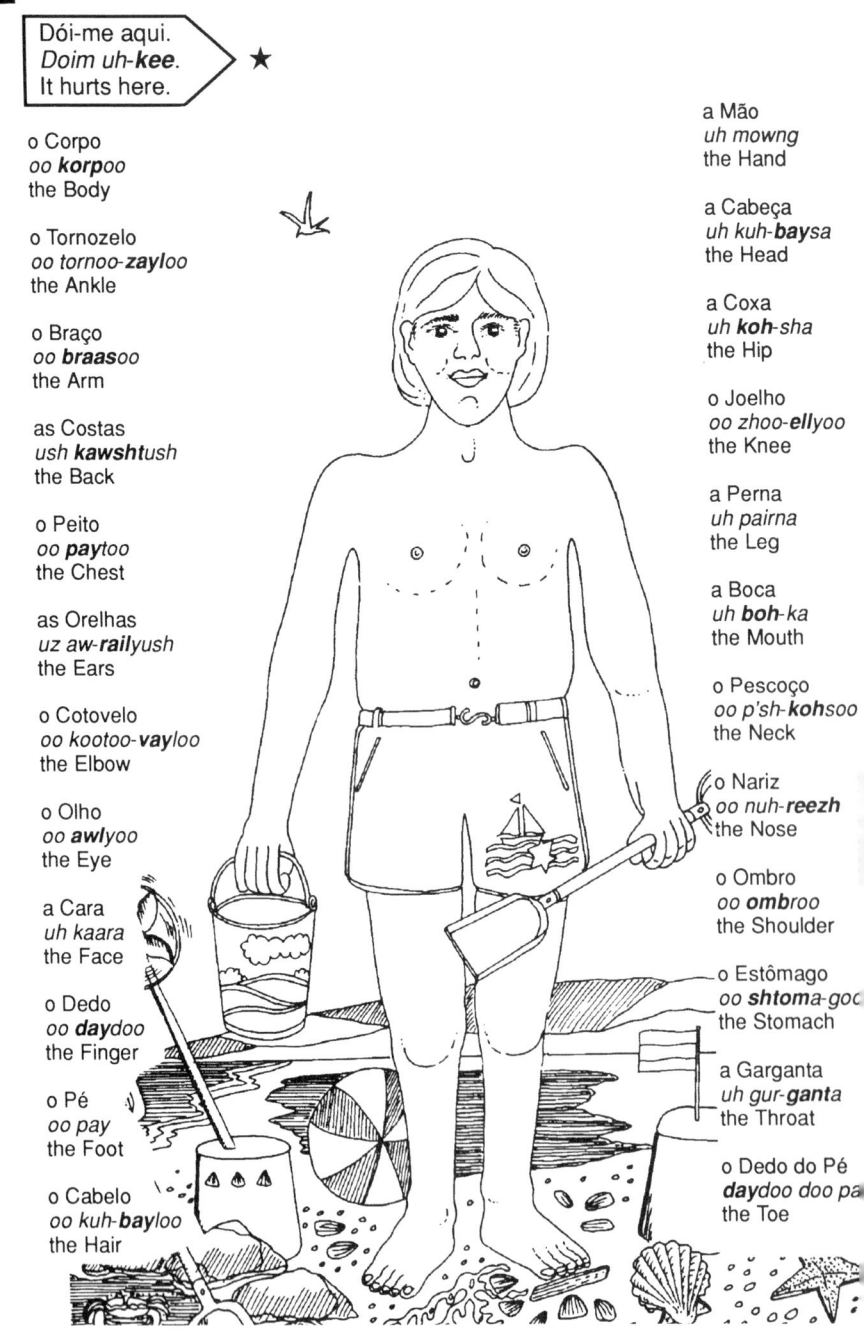

Dói-me aqui.
Doim uh-kee.
It hurts here. ★

o Corpo
oo korpoo
the Body

o Tornozelo
oo tornoo-zayloo
the Ankle

o Braço
oo braasoo
the Arm

as Costas
ush kawshtush
the Back

o Peito
oo paytoo
the Chest

as Orelhas
uz aw-railyush
the Ears

o Cotovelo
oo kootoo-vayloo
the Elbow

o Olho
oo awlyoo
the Eye

a Cara
uh kaara
the Face

o Dedo
oo daydoo
the Finger

o Pé
oo pay
the Foot

o Cabelo
oo kuh-bayloo
the Hair

a Mão
uh mowng
the Hand

a Cabeça
uh kuh-baysa
the Head

a Coxa
uh koh-sha
the Hip

o Joelho
oo zhoo-ellyoo
the Knee

a Perna
uh pairna
the Leg

a Boca
uh boh-ka
the Mouth

o Pescoço
oo p'sh-kohsoo
the Neck

o Nariz
oo nuh-reezh
the Nose

o Ombro
oo ombroo
the Shoulder

o Estômago
oo shtoma-goo
the Stomach

a Garganta
uh gur-ganta
the Throat

o Dedo do Pé
daydoo doo pa
the Toe

Sightseeing

> Onde é o Turismo?
> **Awndy**-ay ooToo-**reezh**moo?
> Where is the Tourist Office?

> 1. O que há de interesse em Évora?
> 2. Há o castelo, o mosteiro, a velha cidade...
> 3. Quando se pode visitar o castelo?
> 4. Pode-se visitar todos os dias excepto às segundas.

1. *Oo kee **a** deen-**trays** eng **Ay**vor-a?*
   What is there to see in Évora?

2. ***A** oo kush-**tel**loo, oo moosh-**tay**roo, uh velya see-**daad***
   There is the castle, the monastery, the old town...

3. ***Kwan**doo s'pod veezy-**tar** oo kush-**tel**loo?*
   When can you visit the castle?

4. *Pods veezy-**tar** toh-doosh dee-ush ish-**set**too ash s'**goond**ush.*
   It's open every day except Monday.

> Pode-se entrar?
> *Podsen-**trar**?*
> Can you go in?

Exposição
Exhibition

Entrada
Entrance

Saída
Exit

> 1. Tem uma planta da cidade, faz favor?
> 2. Há um guia que fale Inglês?

1. *Teng ooma planta d'see-**daad**, fash fuh-**vor**?*
   Have you got a town plan, please?

2. *A oong ghee-a kuh **fal**ay een-**glaysh**?*
   Is there a guide who speaks English?

Sport

1. Onde ficam os campos de ténis?
2. Quanto custa por dia/jogo/hora?
3. Onde é a praia/a piscina?
4. Onde se pode pescar?

Proibido tomar banho
No swimming

1. *Awnd **feek**ang oosh **kamp**oosh d'**tay**neesh?*
   Where are the tennis courts?
2. ***Kwan**too **koosh**ta poor dee-a/**zhoh**-goo/ora?*
   How much is it per day/game/hour?
3. *Awndy-**ay** uh pr-**eye**-a/uh p'sh-**seen**a?*
   Where is the beach/swimming pool?
4. *Awnd s'pod p'sh-**kar**?*
   Where can you go fishing?

Golf

1. Onde é o campo de golfe?
2. Onde se pode...?

Jogar o Golfe
*zhoo-**gar** oo golf*
to Play Golf

as Madeiras
*ush muh-**day**rush*
the Clubs

um 'Handicap'
*oong **hand**icap*
a Handicap

o Buraco
*oo boo-**rak**koo*
the Hole

o Par
oo par
Par

1. *Awndy-**ay** oo **kamp**oo d'gawlf?*
   Where is the golf course?
2. *Awnd s'pod...?*
   Where can you...?

Fazer...	equitação	vela	surfismo	esqui aquático
*fuh-**zair***	*eekeeta-**sowng***	*vaylä*	*soor-**feez**moo*	*shkee uh-**kwatt**y-koo*
Go...	Riding	Sailing	Surfing	Water-skiing

Entertainment: booking tickets

1. Há algum jogo de futebol (alguma tourada) esta semana?
2. Queria dois bilhetes para esta noite (sexta-feira à tarde/noite).
3. Ao sol ou à sombra?
4. Quer um bilhete de — escudos?

1. *A algoong zho-goo d'foot-bawl (algooma toraada) eshta s'maana?*
   Are there any football matches (bullfights) on this week?
2. *Kree-a doish beel-yetsh purra eshta noit (sayshta fayra a tard/noit).*
   I'd like two tickets for this evening (Friday afternoon/evening).
3. *Ow sol oh a sombra?*
   In the sun or the shade?
4. *Kair oong beel-yet d' — shkoodoosh?*
   Do you want a — esc. ticket?

Bilheteira aberta a partir das...
entre as 8h da manhã e as 6h da tarde
Ticket office open from...
between 8am and 6pm

1. Que há esta noite no cinema/teatro?
2. A que horas começa?
3. Há uma discoteca aqui perto?

bancada/fila - row of seats

um lugar de plateia (balcão)

loo-gar duppla-taya (bal-kowng)

one seat in the stalls (circle)

1. *Kuh a eshta noit noo see-nayma/tee-aatroo?*
   What's on at the cinema/theatre tonight?
2. *Uh kee orush koo-messa?*
   When does it start?
3. *A ooma dishkno-tekka uh-kee pairtoo?*
   Is there a disco here?

Meeting people

Speech bubbles (top scene):
1. Olá, está um dia lindo, não está? Como está?
2. Muito bem, obrigado/a. E o senhor (a senhora)?
3. Chamo-me —. Como se chama?
4. Este é o meu marido (a minha mulher), o meu filho (a minha filha) e o meu amigo (a minha amiga).
5. Muito prazer.
6. Igualmente.

1. *Aw-**la**, shta oong dee-a **leen**doo, nowng shta? **Kaw**moo shta?*
   Hallo. What a lovely day! How are you?
2. ***Mween**too beng, obry-**gaa**doo/a. Ee oo s'n-**yor** (uh s'n-**yor**a)?*
   Fine, thanks – and you? (to a man/woman)
3. ***Sham**moom —. **Kaw**moo s'**sham**ma?*
   I'm called —. What's your name?
4. ***Esh**ty-ay oo **may**oo muh-**ree**doo (uh **meen**ya mool-**yair**), oo **may**oo **feel**yoo (uh **meen**ya **feel**ya) ee oo **may**oo uh-**mee**goo (uh **meen**ya uh-**mee**ga).*
   This is my husband/wife, my son/daughter and my friend (male/female).
5. ***Mween**too pruh-**zair**.*
   Pleased to meet you.
6. *Eegwal-**ment**.*
   The same to you.

Speech bubbles (bottom scene):
1. Olá! Sou —.
2. Este é o meu irmão. (Esta é a minha irmã.)
3. Tens irmãos e irmãs?
4. Quantos anos tens?
5. Tenho treze anos.
6. Ciao!/Adeus!

1. *Aw-**la**! So —.*
   Hallo! I'm —.
2. ***Esh**ty-ay oo **may**oo eer-**mowng** (**Esh**ta ay uh **meen**ya eer-**mang**).*
   This is my brother (my sister).
3. *Tainsh eer-**mowng**sh ee eer-**mang**sh?*
   Have you any brothers and sisters?
4. ***Kwan**toosh **unn**oosh tainsh?*
   How old are you?
5. ***Tain**yoo trayz **unn**oosh.*
   I'm 13.*
6. *Chow!/Uh-**day**oosh!*
   Goodbye.

Making friends

> 1. É a primeira vez que vem a Portugal/ao Brasil?
>
> 2. Gosta de estar aqui?
>
> 3. Sim, muito.
>
> 4. Donde é?
>
> 5. Sou de Londres.

1. *Ay uh pree-**may**ra vesh k'**veng** uh Poortoo-**gal**/ow Bruh-**zeel**?*
   Is this your first visit to Portugal/Brazil?
2. *Gawshta dish-**tar** uh-**kee**?*
   Do you like it here?
3. *Sing, **mween**too.*
   Yes, very much.
4. *Dawndy-ay?*
   Where do you come from?
5. *So d'**Lawn**drush.*
   I'm from London.

Accepting an invitation

> 1. Estás livre esta noite?
>
> 2. Gostarias de vir ver-nos? (ver-me)
>
> 3. Estupendo. Adorava.
>
> 4. A que horas nos encontramos?

Portuguese has its own versions of Dublin *(Dublim)*, Edinburgh *(Edimburgo)*, and London *(Londres)*. In Canada there is Newfoundland *(Terra Nova)*, Nova Scotia *(Nova Escócia)*, Ottawa *(Otava)*, and Quebec *(Quebeque)*. Most names in the U.S. are easily recognisable – except *Nova Iorque:* New York.

1. *Shtash leevra eshta noit?*
   Are you free this evening?
2. *Gooshta-**ree**yush d'veer **vair**noosh? (vairm)*
   Would you like to come and see us? (me)
3. *Shtoo **pain**doo. Uddor-**aa**va.*
   That would be very nice, I'd love to.
4. *Uh kee **or**ush noosh ainkon-**tramm**oosh?*
   When shall we meet?

Visiting

1. Olá, que tal?
2. Bem.
3. Senta-te. Serve-te.
4. Gostas de: ler, *desporto, dançar, música?
5. Gosto de...
6. É muito bom.

1. *Aw-la, k'taal?*
   Hello, how are you?
2. *Beng.*
   Fine.
3. ***Sainta**-tuh. **Sairva**-tuh.*
   Sit down. Help yourself.
4. ***Gawsht**ush d': lair, dush**port**oo, dan-**sar**, **moozy**-ka?*
   Do you like: reading, sport, dancing, music?
5. ***Gawsht**oo d'...*
   I like...
6. *Em-**ween**too bong.*
   It tastes very nice.

*Br. *esporte*

Sim, obrigado/a — Não, obrigado/a
Yes, please — No, thank you

Saying goodbye

*In Brazil; in Portugal, within 24 hours

1. Muito obrigado/a por esta noite. Foi estupendo.
2. De nada. Até logo.*
3. Boa noite.

1. ***Mween**too obry-**gaa**doo/a poor eshta noit. Foy shtoo-**pain**doo.*
   Thank you very much for this evening. It was lovely.
2. *D'nadda. Uh-**tay law**goo.*
   Not at all. See you soon.
3. *Boa noit.*
   Goodnight.

My family – A minha família *(a meenya fuh-meelya)*

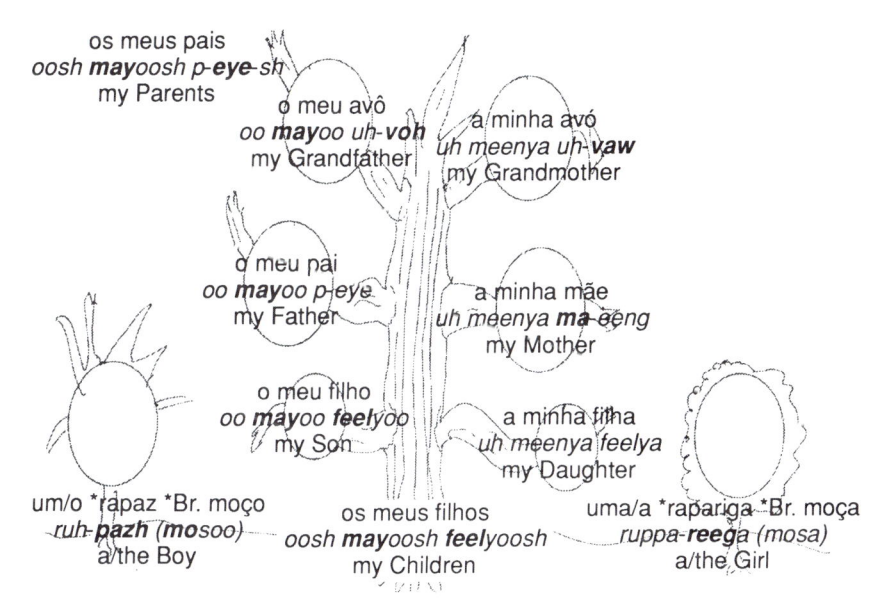

os meus pais
oosh mayoosh p-eye-sh
my Parents

o meu avô
oo mayoo uh-voh
my Grandfather

a minha avó
uh meenya uh-vaw
my Grandmother

o meu pai
oo mayoo p-eye
my Father

a minha mãe
uh meenya ma-eeng
my Mother

o meu filho
oo mayoo feelyoo
my Son

a minha filha
uh meenya feelya
my Daughter

um/o *rapaz *Br. moço
ruh-pazh (mosoo)
a/the Boy

os meus filhos
oosh mayoosh feelyoosh
my Children

uma/a *rapariga *Br. moça
ruppa-reega (mosa)
a/the Girl

Countries and nationalities

Donde é?   Sou de...   Sou português/portuguesa/brasileiro/brasileira
Dawndy-ay?   *So d'...*   *So poortoogaysh/-gayza/braazi-layroo/-layra*
Where are you from?   I'm from   I am Portuguese (man/woman)/Brazilian (m./f.)

Inglaterra	inglês/inglesa	Irlanda	irlandês/irlandesa
eengla-terra	*eeng-laysh/-layza*	*eer-landa*	*eerlandaysh/-dayza*
England	English	Ireland	Irish
Escócia	escocês/escocesa	País de Gales	galês/galesa
shkawsy-a	*shko-saysh/-sayza*	*pa-eesh d'galsh*	*guh-laysh/-layza*
Scotland	Scottish	Wales	Welsh

os Estados Unidos   (norte) americano/a
oosh shtaadoosh oo-needoosh   *(nort) ummurry-kaanoo/a*
the U.S.A.   (North) American

Austrália   australiano/a
owsh-traaly-a   *owsh-traaly-aanoo/a*
Australia   Australian

Canadá   canadiano/a
canna-da   *ca-naddy-aanoo/a*
Canada   Canadian

Nova Zelândia   Sou da Nova Zelândia
nawva zel-landy-a   *so duh nawva zel-landy a*
New Zealand   I'm from New Zealand

Pests

1. Deixe-me em paz!
2. Vá-se embora!
3. Vá passear!

1. **Daysh**meng pash!
   Leave me alone!
2. Vass yem-**bora**!
   Go away!
3. Va pussee-**ar**!
   Get lost!

Theft and lost property

1. Perdi (o meu passaporte).
2. Roubaram-me (a minha mala).
3. Como é? O que tinha lá dentro?

1. Pur-**dee** (oo **may**oo passa-**port**).
   I've lost (my passport).
2. Roh-**bar**um m' (uh **mee**nya **maa**la).
   (My bag) has been stolen.
3. **Kaw**moo ay? Oo k'**teen**ya la **dain**troo?
   What does it look like? What was in it?

a minha Máquina Fotográfica	**mee**nya **makk**y-na foto**graff**y-ka	my Camera
o meu Dinheiro	**may**oo deen-**yay**roo	my Money
os meus Cheques de Viagem	**may**oosh shaiksh d'vee-**aazh**eng	my Traveller's Cheques

Nome	Apelido/Br.Sobrenome	Endereço	Quando	Onde
nawm	up-**leed**oo	ain-**dray**soo	**kwan**doo	awnd
1st Name	Surname	Address	When	Where

}?

Seasons, months and weather

na primavera	*na preema-**vaira***	in Spring

	faz vento *fash **vain**too* it's Windy		chove *shawv* it's Raining	
Março ***mar**soo* MARCH	a Páscoa *uh **pash**kwa* Easter	Abril *uh-**breel*** APRIL		Maio ***my**-oo* MAY

no verão	*noo v'**rowng***	in Summer

	faz sol *fash sol* it's Sunny		faz calor *fash kuh-**lor*** it's Hot	
Junho ***zhoon**-yoo* JUNE		Julho ***zhool**-yoo* JULY	tenho calor *tainyoo kuh-**lor*** I'm Hot	Agosto *uh-**gosh**too* AUGUST

no outono	*noo oh-**tawn**oo*	in Autumn/Fall

	a vindima *uh veen-**deem**a* the Wine Harvest		faz frio *fash free oo* it's Cold	
Setembro *s'**taim**broo* SEPTEMBER		Outubro *oh-**too**broo* OCTOBER	tenho frio *tainyoo free-oo* I'm Cold	Novembro *noo-**vaim**broo* NOVEMBER

no inverno	*noo een-**vair**noo*	in Winter

	Feliz Natal *f'**leesh** nuh-**taal*** Happy Christmas		e Próspero Ano Novo *ee **prosh**proo **ah**noo **nov**oo* and a prosperous New Year	
Dezembro *d'**zaim**broo* DECEMBER	neva *nayva* it's Snowing	Janeiro *zhuh-**nay**roo* JANUARY		Fevereiro *fuv-**ray**roo* FEBRUARY

Time of day   Greetings

ontem
awnteng
Yesterday

hoje
awzh
Today

amanhã
ammun-yang
Tomorrow

agora
uh-gora
Now

Bom dia
bong dee-a
Good Morning

Boa tarde
boa tard
Good afternoon/evening (till sunset)

Boa noite
boa noit
Good night (after dark)

a manhã
uh mun-yang
the Morning

a tarde
uh tard
the Afternoon/Evening

a noite
uh noit
the Night

Days of the week

segunda-feira
s'goonda fayra
Monday

terça-feira
tairsa fayra
Tuesday

quarta-feira
kwarta fayra
Wednesday

quinta-feira
keenta fayra
Thursday

sexta-feira
sayshta fayra
Friday

sábado
sabba-doo
Saturday

domingo
doo-meengoo
Sunday

uma semana
ooma s'maana
a Week

Time

Que horas são? *kee **o**rush sowng?* What's the time?

uma hora — *ooma ora* — an hour
meia-hora — *maya ora* — half an hour
um quarto de hora — *oong **kwar**too dee ora* — a quarter of an hour

São <u>três</u>
sowng traysh
It's <u>three o'clock</u>

três <u>e cinco</u>
*traysh ee **seen**koo*
<u>five past</u> three

quatro <u>e dez</u>
***kwat**roo ee desh*
<u>ten past</u> four

cinco <u>e um quarto</u>
***seen**koo ee oong **kwar**too*
<u>quarter past</u> five

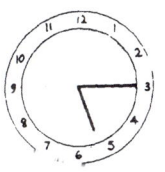

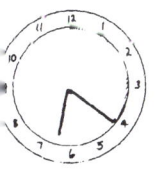

seis <u>e vinte</u>
saysh ee veent
<u>twenty past</u> six

sete <u>e vinte e cinco</u>
*set ee veenty **seen**koo*
<u>twenty-five past</u> seven

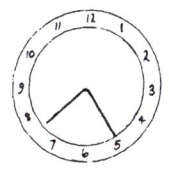

oito <u>e meia</u>
oitoo ee maya
<u>half past</u> eight

<u>vinte e cinco para as</u> nove
*veenty **seen**koo purra ush nawv*
<u>twenty-five to</u> nine

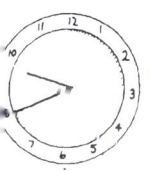

<u>vinte para as</u> dez
veent purra ush desh
<u>twenty to</u> ten

<u>um quarto para as</u> onze
*oong **kwar**too purra ush awnz*
<u>quarter to</u> eleven

<u>dez para</u> o meio-dia/ a meia-noite
*desh purra oo **may**oo dee-a/ uh maya noit*
<u>ten to</u> midday/midnight

***seen**koo purra uh ooma*
<u>cinco para</u> a uma
<u>five to</u> one

72 How Portuguese works

Things: nouns In Portuguese everything is thought of as either masculine (m.) or feminine (f.).

For one thing only, i.e. a **singular** item (s.), **a** is *um* (m.) or *uma* (f.):
um rádio a radio, *uma casa* a house
If there is more than one, i.e. **plural** (pl.), *um* becomes *uns*, *uma* becomes *umas*.
uns rádios some radios, *umas casas* some houses

The is *o* for masculine words: *o rádio* the radio, (plural *os)*
a for feminine ones: *a casa* the house, (plural *as)*

Nouns ending in a vowel add *-s: os rádios* the radios, *as casas* the houses.
Other nouns change according to their endings:
-al, el, -ol become *-ais, -éis, -is, -óis: o jornal, os jornais* newspaper/s,
 o pastel, os pastéis cake/s, *o lençol, os lençóis* sheet/s
-ão usually changes to *-ões: a estação, as estações* station/s; sometimes
 -ães: o cão, os cães dog/s; or may just add *-s: a mão, as mãos* hand/s
-il when stressed becomes *-is: o barril, os barris* barrel/s;
 unstressed *-eis: o têxtil, os têxteis* textile/s
-m changes to *ns: o homem, os homens* man/men
-r, -s/-ís, -z add *-es: a mulher* (woman), *as mulheres* ; *o país* (country), *os países*

Describing words: adjectives
Adjectives usually follow the nouns they describe. If it is masculine, the adjective will be too. If it is feminine or plural, the ending will change accordingly:
 o vinho branco the white wine   *os vinhos brancos* the white wines
 a casa branca the white house   *as casas brancas* the white houses
Adjectives ending in *-e (verde* – green) or a consonant *(azul* – blue) do not change.
Other exceptions: *português/portuguesa, bom/boa* (good), *mau/má* (bad).

*Obrigado/obrigada means literally 'obliged', i.e. 'thank you.' For this reason, a man will say *obrigado* while for a woman it's *obrigada*.

In, on, at, to: prepositions These contract when used with *o* and *a* (the):

	o	a	os	as			o	a	os	as
a to, at	ao	à	aos	às	**em**	in, on	no	na	nos	nas
de of, from	do	da	dos	das	**por**	by, for	pelo	pela	pelos	pelas

de and *em* also contract with *um/uma: dum/duma* (of/from a), *num/numa* (in/on a)

It's mine: possessives
Unlike English, 'my,' 'your,' etc. agree in number and gender with what is possessed.

	m. sing.	pl.	f. sing.	pl.
my	o meu	os meus	a minha	as minhas
our	o nosso	os nossos	a nossa	as nossas
your (você/s), his, her, its, their	o seu	os seus	a sua	as suas

People or things: pronouns

'I,' 'you' *(eu, tu),* etc. are only used for emphasis or to avoid ambiguity since the verb ending shows who is meant. You will generally use the third person of the verb (the same as 'he,' 'she,' 'it') to mean 'you,' e.g. *Fala inglês?* – Do you speak English?

If you need to be specific when talking to a stranger, you can say *o senhor* or *a senhora* (plural *os senhores/as senhoras*): *O senhor fala inglês?* – Does the gentleman speak English? When you know someone better you can address them as *você (**voss**ay),* plural *vocês: Você fala inglês? (Você* and *os senhores* etc. all use the third person.) *Tu* is used with family and close friends.

Doing words: verbs

Portuguese has two verbs 'to be.' *Ser* is for a permanent condition or something immovable, e.g. *Sou inglês* – I am English; *Onde é o banco?* – Where is the bank? *Estar* is for something that is temporary or movable, e.g. *Como está?* – How are you? *Onde está o carro?* – Where is the car?

to be		*ser*	*estar*
I am	*(eu)*	*sou*	*estou*
you are	*(tu)*	*és*	*estás*
you are (polite s.)	*(você, o sr/a sr*a*)}*	*é*	*está*
he, she, it is	*(ele, ela) }*		
we are	*(nós)*	*somos*	*estamos*
you are (polite pl.)	*(vocês, os srs/as sr*as*)}*	*são*	*estão*
they are	*(eles, elas) }*		

to have	*ter*	**to want**	*querer*
I have	*tenho*	I want	*quero*
you have *(tu)*	*tens*	you want *(tu)*	*queres*
você etc. have }	*tem*	*você* etc. want }	*quer*
he, she, it has }		he, she, it wants}	
we have	*temos*	we want	*queremos*
vocês &c, they have	*têm*	*vocês* &c, they want	*querem*

to go	*ir*	**to be able**	*poder*
I go	*vou*	I can	*posso*
you go *(tu)*	*vais*	you can *(tu)*	*podes*
você etc go }	*vai*	*você* etc can }	*pode*
he, she, it goes}		he, she, it can}	
we go	*vamos*	we can	*podemos*
vocês etc, they go	*vão*	*vocês* etc, they can	*podem*

Saying no
Put *não* in front of the verb: *Não posso.* I can't. *Não sei.* I don't know.

Questions Just speak the sentence as if it were a question:
(Você) fala inglês. You speak English. *(Você) fala inglês?* Do you speak English?

Portuguese index/food terms

Aberto/a	open
Açorda	bread soup
Água mineral	mineral water
Alface	lettuce
Alheira	garlic sausage
Alho	garlic
Almoço/s	lunch/es
Almondegas	meatballs
Ameijoas	clams, cockles
Ameixas	plums
Amêndoa	almond
Ananás	pineapple
A partir da	from
Arroz; doce	rice; -pudding
" de marisco	seafood paella
A/s	to
Assado/a	roast
Atum	tuna
Bacalhau	**salt cod**
Batatas; fritas	potatoes; chips/crisps
uma Bifana	hot pork roll
Bife	beef; steak-shape
um Bitoque	small steak, egg, chips
um Bolo, de noz	cake, walnut-
Borrego	lamb
Branco	white
à Brás	+ onions, potatoes, egg
na Brasa	barbecued
Cabrito	**kid**
um Cachorro	hot dog
Cachucho	bream
em Calda	in syrup
Caldeirada	fish stew
Caldo verde	cabbage soup
Camarão,-ões	prawn/s
Canja de galinha	chicken broth
Carapau	horse-mackerel
Carneiro	mutton
Carnes; -frias	meat; beef; cold-
da Casa, Caseiro	house speciality
Cebola	onion
Cenoura	carrot
Cerejas	cherries
uma Cerveja	beer
Chá	tea
Chocos	squid
um Chouriço	smoked sausage
no Churrasco	barbecued
Coco	coconut
Coelho	rabbit
Cogumelos	mushrooms
Com	with
Combinados	one-dish meals
Comidas	meals
Codorniz	quail
Cozido	stew; boiled
Da/s	**from**
Descascado	shelled, peeled
Dobrada	tripe
Doce	dessert
Empada, -ão	pie, large-
Ervas	green vegetables
Ervilhas	peas
Espadarte	large swordfish
Espargos	asparagus
Espeto; espetada	on the spit; kebab
Estrelado	fried
Farófias	**milk, eggwhite, custard**
Favas	broad beans
Febras	lean meat
Feijão, verde/frade	bean, green/black-eye
Feijoada	bean & meat stew
Fiambre	ham
Fígado	liver
Filetes	fillets
no Forno	baked
Frango assado	roast chicken
" no churrasco	barbecued
na Frigideira	fried + ham & wine
Frito	fried
Fruta	fruit
Gambas	**prawns**
Gaspacho	cold tomato soup
um Gelado	ice cream
à Gomes de Sá	+ olives, potatoes, egg
Grão	chickpeas
Grelhado	grilled
Grelos	turnip tops
Há	**there is/are**
uma Hamburga	hamburger
Hortaliça	vegetable
Jantar/es	dinner/s
Lagosta	**lobster**
Laranja	orange
Legumes	vegetables
Leitão	sucking pig
Limão	lemon
Linguado	sole
Lombo, -inho	rump, tenderloin
Lulas	squid
Maçã	**apple**
Manhã	morning
Manteiga	butter
Mariscos	seafood
Marmelo, -ada	quince, -conserve
Massas	pasta
Melão	melon
Mexilhões	mussels
Misto/a	mixed
Molho	sauce
(Pudim) Molotov	egg whites, caramel
Morangos	strawberries
Nata	**cream; custard**
ao Natural	plain
Novilho	beef

Omeleta	**omelette**
Ovos, mexidos	eggs, scrambled-
" moles	candied egg yolks
Paio	**smoked sausage**
Pão; de Ló	bread; rich sponge cake
Pasta	pâté
Pastel, /-eis	cake/s; vol-au-vent
Peito	breast
Peixe (espada)	(scabbard) fish
Pera	pear
Perú	turkey
Pescada	hake
Pêssego	peach
Picado	minced
Pimentos	peppers
Piri-piri	hot chilli sauce
Polvo	octopus
Porco à Alentejana	pork with clams
à Portuguesa	+ tomatoes, onions
Prato do dia	dish of the day
um Prego; no prato	steak roll;+ fried egg
Presunto	smoked ham
Pudim de chá	tea cream
" flan	caramel cream
Queijo	**cheese**
Quinta	farm, estate
Recheado	**stuffed**
Rissóis	rissoles
Rojões	kidneys
Russo/a	diced vegetables
Salada; mista	**salad; mixed**
Salgados	salted snacks
Salmão	salmon
Salmonetes	red mullet
Salsa	parsley
Salsicha	sausage
uma Sandes	sandwich
uma Sanduíche	sandwich
Santola	spider crab
Sarapatel	haggis
Sarda	mackerel
Sardinhas	sardines
Sem	without
Simples	plain
Só	only
Sobremesa	dessert
Solho	plaice
Sopa	soup
um Sorvete	ice cream (Br.)
um Suco	fruit juice (Br.)
um Sumo	fruit juice
Tarde	**afternoon, evening**
Tinto; tinta	red; ink (squid)
Torrado/a	toast
Torta	tart, pie; sponge roll
uma Tosta	toasted sandwich
" mista	" + ham, cheese

Index 75

Toucinho	belly pork
Toucinho do ceu	almonds, eggs, sugar
Tripas	tripe
Truta	trout
Uvas	**grapes**
Vaca	**beef**
Vende-se para fora	take-away
Vitela, -linha	veal

Index

Accident	38,57
Address	68
Aeroplane	56
After	39,59
Again	81
Age	7,58,64
Air	46
Airport	56
Allergic	59
Ambulance	57
American, etc.	67
Antiseptic cream	30
Apartment	12
Appointment	57,59
Arrival	50,56
Aspirin	30
Asthmatic	59
Awning	7
Baby food	30
Bad	72
Bag	28,68
Baggage	51
Baker	24
Bandage, Band-Aid	30
Bank	35-36
Bath/room	7,9,13
Battery	31
Be/be able	8,73
Beach	40,55,62
Bed/room	8,9,10,13,15
Beer	10,17,25
Before	39,59
Behind	39
Belt	34
Better	11
Bicycle, parts	42,48,49
Big	21,24,33,45
Bill, hotel	11
restaurant	17,22
Biscuit	25
Bite	32,58
Blood pressure	59
Boat	55
Body	60
Book	7,18,31,56
Booking, campsite	7,14-15

Index

entertainment	63	Corkscrew	31
flight	56	Corner	39
hostel	15	Cost	23,33,81
hotel, room	7,8-11	Cotton, -wool	30,31
letter	7	Couchette	52
restaurant	18	Cough	32
train	50,52	Countries	67,72
Bottle/opener	22,31	Crash helmet	49
Boy	67	Credit card	33
Brazil, -ian	3,65,67	Crossroads	39
Bread	18,22,24	Cup	12,13,17,18
Breakdown	47,48	Customs	81
Breakfast	8,11,16,18	Cutlery	13,22
Bridge	40		
Bring	18	**Dam**	40
Britain	37,38	Dancing	66
Broken	12,48	Danger	55
Brother	64	Daughter	64,67
Bullfight	63	Day	45,51,57,59,62,64,70
Bus	54	Dentist	59
Butter	18,25	Deodorant	30
		Departure	50,54,56
Café	16,17	Dessert	19,20
Cake	16,17,72	Diabetic	59
Called	10,21,64	Diaper	30
Camera	68	Diarrhoea	32
Camping, -Gaz	7,14-15,31	Dictionary	31
Can, be able	8,11,62,73,81	Direct	56
Cancel	56	Directions	39
Can opener	31	Disco	63
Car:	7,42-49	Doctor	57
hire	45	Dollar	33,36
parts	48,49	Door	12
Caravan	7,14	Drink, to	22,58
Castle	40,61	Drinks	17,22
Casualty Department	57	Driving licence	45
Cathedral	40	Drugstore	30,32
Chair	13		
Change	36,53,56	**Earache**	32
Cheers!	16	Easter	69
Cheese	17,23,25	Eat	16,58
Chemist	30,32	Egg	25
Cheque	33,36,68	Electricity	7,12,15
Child	7,9,14,19,34,64,67	Emergency	38,44,47,57
Chips/fries	19,20	English, etc.	61,67,81
Chocolate	18,21	Enough	23
Choosing	21	Entrance	61
Christmas	69	Epileptic	59
Church	40	Evening	15,63,65
Cigarette	31	Every	55,57,59
Cinema	40,63	Excuse me	12,14,18,46,81
Close	15,23	Exhibition	61
Clothes	32-34	Exit	44,61
Coffee	13,17,18,25	Expensive	33
Cold	12,18,69	Expressway	44
Colours	cover,17,32,72	Extension	38
Comb	30		
Come	65,67	**Family**	7,64,67
Complaint	22	Far	39
Condom	30	Father	67
Constipation	32	Film	31
Cookies	25	Find: a seat	53

Index

the way	39
Fire, -Brigade	14,38
First Aid	57
First/second, etc.	65,80
Fish, fishing	16,20,27,62
Fit	33
Flashlight	31
Flat	12,49
Flight	56
Football	63
Free	10,17,53,65
Friend	64,65
Fries	19,20
Fruit:	23,29
-juice	17,25
Fuel	46
Full	8
Fuse	48
Garage	47
Gas, -station	12,31,46
Get off, -to	54,56
Girl	67
Give *dar*	10
Glass	13,17,22
Go	52,54,55,61,73
Go away	68
Golf	62
Good	10,11,66,72,81
Goodbye	23,64,66,81
Good morning, etc.	15,23,70,81
Groceries	23,25
Group	7
Guide	61
Half *meio*	23
Hamburger	17
Handkerchief	30
Harbour	55
Have	11,15,23,73,81
Hay fever	32
Headache	32
Health centre	57
Heart	59
Hello	17,64,66,81
Help	57,66
Here	39
Hill	40
Hobbies	66
Holidays	35
Hospital	57
Hot	12,10,69
Hot dog	17
Hotel	7,8-11,40
Hour	59,62,71
House	72
How are you	64,66
How long	14,15,55,58
How many/much	9,10,23,45,62,81
Hungry	16
Hurt	58,60
Husband	64
Ice, -cream	16,17,21
-pack	31
Ill, illness	32,57,59
Information	51,61
Insect bite	32,58
-repellant	30
Introductions	64
Invitation	65
Island	55
Jam	25
(Good) Journey	42
Jug	13
Key	10,12,49
Kitchen	12,13
Knife, etc.	13
Know	73,81
Lake	55
Lavatory	9,13,17,39
Leak	49
Leave	54
Left	39
Left luggage	51
Letter	7,37
Life belt/boat/jacket	55
Lift	8
Light/bulb	13,48,49
Like	9,11,18,33,65,66,81
Like this	24
Line	38,53
Live	12,65
Locations	39
Look like	68
Looking (just)	23
Lose, lost	68,81
Lost property	68
Lovely	64,66
Luggage	49,51
Mall	37
Man	72
Map	31,39,61
Margarine	25
Market	23,40
Marmalade	18
Match	31
Matter	47,81
Me	65
Meal/times	8,11,16,59
Mean	81
Measure/s	27,32
Meat	17,19,20,23,26
Medicine	30,32,58,59
Meet	64,65
Membership card	15
Mend	12,47
Menu	16,19
Midday/night	71
Milk	10,25
Mistake	22

Index

Monastery	61	Portugal, Portuguese	3,65,67,72,81
Money	36,68	Postcard	31,37
Months	69	Post Office	37
More	12,22	Pregnant	59
Morning	59,70	Prescription	58
Mother	67	Price	23,33,62,81
Motorcycle, parts	42,48,49	Public holidays	35
Motorway	44	Puncture	49
Movie	63		
Mr, Mrs	12,38,73	**Quantities**	23,27
Museum	40	Questions	22,73
Music	66	Quiet (noisy)	11
Must	53		
My	72	**Radio** *o rádio*	72
		Rain	69
Name	10,21,64,68	Razor	30
Nappy	30	Reading	66
Nationality	67	Repair	12,46,47
Near, -est	8,39,46,47	Repeat	81
Need	48,53	Request	22
Needle	31	Reservation – see Booking	
Newspaper	31,72	Restaurant	16,18-22
New Year	69	Return	52
Next, -to	39,56	Rice	25
Nice	22,64,65,66	Riding	62
Night	7,9,32,59,70	Right	39
No, not	11,66,73,81	River	40
Noisy	11	Road, -signs	39,43-44
North, etc.	41	Roll	18,24
Nothing	81	Room	7,9,11
Now	70	Rope	31
Number/s	10,56,80	Round trip	52
Nut	29,49	Rubbish	13,14
Occupied	17,39,53	**Sailing**	55,62
Oil	25,46,49	Salad	19,20
OK	9,22,23,81	Sale	33
Old	58,64	Salt & pepper	25
Olives	28	Sandwich	16,17
Open, -times	23,46,61,63	Sanitary napkin/towel	30
Opposite	39	Scissors	31
Overheating	48	Screw, -driver	49
		Sea, -sick	32,55
Pan	13	Seafood	16,27
Pardon	81	Seasons	69
Park	40,42	Seat	52,53,63
Parking	10,42	See	65,66
Passport	8,68	Self-catering	12-13
Pasta	25	Self-service	21
Paying	11,17,33,58	Shade	7,63
Pen, pencil	31	Shampoo	30
Person	7,9,14	Shop	23,41,46
Pests	68	Shower	7,9
Petrol, -station	46	Sick	32,57,58,59
Place names	3,65	Sightseeing	61
Plaster	30	Single	7,9,52
Plate	13	Sister	67
Platform	50,52	Sit	63
Please(d)	64,66,81	Size	33
Police	38,40	Sleeper	52
Port	22,55	Sleeping bag	14
Portion *dose*	16	Slice	24

Index

Slow	81
Small	11,21,23,24,33,45
Smoking	31,52,53
Snack	17
Snow	69
Soap, -liquid, -powder	25,30
Son	64,67
Soon	66
Sorry	11,81
Soup	19,20
Speak	38,61,73,81
Speed limits	43
Spell, write	81
Sport	62,66
Square	36,41
Stall (to)	48
Stamp	31,37
Station	50-52,54,72
Stay	14,15
Steak	19,26
Sting	32,58
Stolen	68
Stomach, -ache	32,60
Stop	51,54
Straight on	39
Strap	49
Street, -map	31,41
String	31
Subway	53
Sugar	17,25
Summer, etc.	69
Sun	63,69
Sunburn	32
Sunglasses, -oil	30
Supermarket	23
Surfing	62
Swimming	34,62
Take, -away	11,16,17,33
Tampon	30
Taxi	42
Tea, -room	16,17,25
Telephone	38,44,47
Television *o televisor*	
Temperature	58,59
Tennis	62
Tent	7,14
Tetanus	58
Thank you	47,66,72,81
Theatre	41,63
Theft	68
There	39
There is/are *há*	7,8,38,61
(I) Think so *acho que sim*	6
Thirsty	16
This, that	21,23,24
Thread	31
Throat, sore-	32,60
Ticket: entertainment	61,63
transport	50,52,53,56
Time	11,18,59,61,70,71
Timetable	50,51
Tin opener	31
Tipping	16
Toast	18
Today	63,70
Toilet	13,17,39
-paper	25
Toll	44
Tools	49
Tomorrow	70
Tonight	9,63,65
Toothache	59
Toothbrush, -paste	30
Torch	31
Tourist office	8,41,61
Towel	13
Town; -hall	40,61
Train	50-53
Tram	54
Trash	13,14
Try on	33
Tyre	46,49
Understand	81
Urgent	57
U.S. etc.	37,67
Us	65
Vaccinated	58
Vegetable	19,20,21,23,28
Vegetarian	19
Very *muito*	65
Visit	61,65,66
Walk	42
Want, like	18,23,33,73,81
Water	12,14,22,25,46,49
Water skiing	62
Way out	50,61
W.C.	13,17,39
Weather	64,69
Week	9,14,45,70
Weight	23,27
What	19,47,68,81
When	12,52,61,68,81
Where	10,38,41,68,81
Which	52,53
Who, why	81
Wife	64
Wind	69
Window	13
Windsurfing	62
Wine	17,22,25,69,72
Winter	69
With *com*	7,18
Woman	72
(Not) working	12,48
Write	81
Year	64
Yes	65,66,81
Yesterday	70
Yogurt	25
You, your	64,72,73
Youth hostel	15

Numbers

0 zero *zayroo*	17 dezassete *d'za-set*	500 quinhentos *keen-yaintoosh*
1 um/uma *oong/ooma*	18 dezoito *d'zoitoo*	1000 mil *meel*
2 dois/duas *doish/doo-ush*	19 dezanove *d'za-nawv*	5000 cinco mil *seenkoo meel*
3 três *traysh*	20 vinte *veent*	1000 000 um milhão *oong meel-yowng*
4 quatro *kwatroo*	21 vinte e um/uma *veenty oong...*	
5 cinco *seenkoo*	22 vinte e dois/duas *veenty doish...*	1st primeiro/a (m/f) *pree-mayroo/a*
6 seis *saysh*	30 trinta *treenta*	2nd segundo/a *s'goondoo/a*
7 sete *set*	40 quarenta *kwa-renta*	3rd terceiro/a *tur-sayroo/a*
8 oito *oitoo*	50 cinquenta *seen-kwenta*	4th quarto/a *kwartoo/a*
9 nove *nawv*	60 sessenta *s'senta*	5th quinto/a *keentoo/a*
10 dez *desh*	70 setenta *s'tenta*	6th sexto/a *sayshtoo/a*
11 onze *awnz*	80 oitenta *oy-tenta*	7th sétimo/a *setty-moo/a*
12 doze *dawz*	90 noventa *noo-venta*	8th oitavo/a *oy-taavoo/a*
13 treze *trayz*	100 cem *seng*	9th nono/a *nawnoo/a*
14 catorze *kuh-torz*	101 cento e um/uma *saintoo ee oong...*	10th décimo/a *dessy-moo/a*
15 quinze *keenz*	200 duzentos *doo-zaintoosh*	11th décimo/a primeiro/a *dessymoo/a* *preemayroo/a*
16 dezasseis *d'za-saysh*	400 quatrocentos *kwatroo-saintoosh*	